There's No

The Complete Guide to Home Care

Greg Banks

Owner, Angel Alliance Caregivers

Permission to reproduce or transmit in any form or by any means, electronic or mechanical, including photocopying and recording, or by an information storage and retrieval system, must be obtained by contacting the author.

—Disclaimer—
While the author has used his best efforts in preparing this book, the author makes no representation or warranties with respect to accuracy or completeness of the contents of this book. The advice and strategies contained herein may not be suitable for your situation. You should consult a professional where appropriate. The author shall not be liable for any loss of profit or any other special, incidental, consequential or other damages. The purchaser or reader of this publication assumes responsibility for the use of these materials and information. Adherence to all applicable laws and regulations, both advertising and all other aspects of doing business in the United States or any other jurisdiction, is the sole responsibility of the purchaser of reader.

ISBN-13: 978-1517352066
ISBN-10: 1517352061

© Copyright 2015. All Rights Reserved.

Angel Alliance Caregivers

Physical Address: 703 West White Horse Pike, Galloway, New Jersey 08205

Mailing Address: P.O. Box 242, Cologne, New Jersey 08213

609-965-0028
AngelAllianceCaregivers.com
Greg@AngelAllianceCaregivers.com
Info@AngelAllianceCaregivers.com

www.PaperbackExpert.com

What People Say About Angel Alliance Caregivers

All testimonials are faithfully reproduced as originally provided.

"Gratitude has a faithful memory." Thank you so much for your help. The caregiver was a perfect fit for our situation. God Bless your work. I will always recommend your service.
– Christine M.

Angel Alliance Caregivers has been such a blessing and help to me and my mother. Thank you very much!
– Virginia M.

Thanks for helping to take care of my father. We really appreciate all you and the caregivers do throughout the year.
– T. B.

I am a man of few words, but I had to say THANK YOU for all your agency has done!
– Rick M.

"Professional, Kind and Compassionate Care" We needed around the clock care for my 94 year old Grandmother who was in the last months of her life. She was able to remain in her home because of the wonderful care she received from Angel Alliance

Caregivers. The director, Greg Banks, was always available, day or night, to handle questions or concerns. He is very personable and knowledgeable. The staff was caring and compassionate from the beginning of our service until after my Grandmother's passing. Her caregiver even attended her viewing and funeral. What lovely people to meet during such a difficult time.
– S.L.

Thank you for all your help and support in caring for my mom. She really appreciates all the help her caregiver provides and looks forward to her visits!
– J.M.

I wanted to thank you so much for your kindness and compassion to my grand mom, to me and to my family during my Grandmothers care. You were always available (without complaint!) to listen, to provide a solution or to offer reassurance. I truly don't know how we would have handled those months without you and your agency. On behalf of my entire family, THANK YOU for everything! Your kindness has meant so much to us during such a difficult time.
– S.S.

You are the best.... Our family wanted to tell you how pleased we were with Angel Alliance Caregivers. The women that were helping our mother were absolutely wonderful. They all went above and beyond what we were expecting. You could tell that they had a real heart for helping our mother. They showed it by their actions and attitudes. The owner of the agency was

always available to answer any questions or just to lend a caring ear. We felt like we were talking to a friend of the family and not the owner of the agency.
– Dorothy T.

A huge thank you to Angel Alliance Caregivers. They have allowed my parents to stay in the home they have been in for the last 50 years. My brothers and I are in the role as long distance caregivers as none of us live in New Jersey. I know that they are happy and well taken care of. I can call Greg at any time. He has been through this process with his own parents so he knows the anxiety that we are going through. He has a real heart for what he does and it shows in his staff how he runs the agency. I have known him over a year now and think of him more as a friend. His advice and willingness to just listen have been invaluable.
– Judy and Family F.

Table of Contents

Preface 1
Chapter 1: Signs Home Care is Needed 11
    Take the Path of Least Resistance 15

Chapter 2: What IS Home Care? 17
    Home Health Care 18
    Hospice Care 18
    Private Duty Home Care 19
    Recuperative Care 20
    Continuing Care 20
    Licensing of Home Care Agencies 20

Chapter 3: Why Is Home Care the Preferred Choice? 23
    10 Reasons for Home Care 23

Chapter 4: What is the Goal? 27
Chapter 5: At MY Home? 33
    Relationship and Arrangements 33
    Bathroom 36
    Bedroom 36
    Alzheimer's Disease 37
    "Hospital" Accessories 38
    Mobility 38
    Alternatives to Home Care 38

Chapter 6: Planning for Discharge 43
    Who 44
    What and Where 45
    When 46
    How 47

Chapter 7: What Questions to Ask 49
    10 Vital Signs 49

Chapter 8: The Risks in Hiring Through a "Caregiver Registry" 55
    The Traps 55
    Employee-Employer Relationships 56

Payroll Taxes 56
Workers Compensation Versus Home Owners Insurance 57
The Horror Stories 57
Supervision 58
The Bottom Line 58

Chapter 9: Geriatric Care Managers 61
The Bottom Line 64

Chapter 10: Pride, Independence and Money 65
Pride 65
Independence 66
Money 68

Chapter 11: Fall Prevention Tips 71
Keep moving 71
Wear sensible shoes 71
Remove home hazards 72
Light up your living space 73
Use assistive devices 73

Chapter 12: Bathrooms Can Be Dangerous 75

Chapter 13: Family Dynamics 79
Pigeons 79
Bears 81
Turtles 82

Chapter 14: How to Take Those Keys 83
Practical Suggestions 85

Chapter 15: Loneliness 89

Chapter 16: Why Wii? 91

Chapter 17: The Benefits of Bingo 95
Concentration 95
Coordination 96
Stimulus 96
Social Benefits 97

Chapter 18: Paying for Home Care 99
Private Pay 99
Long-Term Care Insurance 99
Medicare 100
Medicaid 101
Health Insurance 101

Other Options 101

Chapter 19: Long-Term Care Insurance 103
Chapter 20: The 4 Parts of Medicare 105
What isn't covered? 106

Chapter 21: Gifts for Caregivers 107
House Cleaning Service 107
Entertainment Gift Card 107
Day Spa Day 107
Netflix or Amazon 108
Coupon for Respite 108
A Book of Encouragement 108
A Note on Employees 108

Chapter 22: Veterans Benefits 111
What is Aid and Attendance? 111
Aid and Attendance Qualifications 112
Applying for Aid and Attendance 112

Appendix 1: Licensing and Certification of Home Care Agencies 115
Appendix 2: Glossary of Terms 119
Appendix 3: Questions to Ask When Choosing a Home Care Company 133
About The Author 137

Preface

I was born in north Jersey in the town of Nutley. I graduated from Nutley High School and attended Rutgers University, but didn't get into senior care at that point. Actually, my career began in the investment field. Over the years I did investments, insurance, financial sales, leasing sales. Still nothing related to home care!

The closest thing to home care in those years is the involvement I had with seniors in my first job. Working with investments at a bank, I found myself interacting with a lot of seniors, advising them about their investments. I really enjoyed working with them. With seniors you knew where they were coming from; they were down-to-earth and a lot of fun. I really enjoyed that.

Greg Banks

Let's fast forward to 2007. My dad was diagnosed with cancer and passed away. Shortly thereafter, my mom was diagnosed with cancer and began to need home care. She still lived in the town of Nutley where she had raised me, while I lived a few hours to the south. My only brother Keith worked in Manhattan and was very busy with work and kids. We suddenly needed to find outside help for Mom. At that time, neither of us knew anything about home care. Leaving the hospital, we were given a list of agencies by the staff, but no one really told us anything. We were left to our own to figure this all out.

My mom lived in a three-level home, with the bedrooms upstairs, the living area downstairs, and the washer and dryer in the basement. She was no longer able to go up and down the stairs. So we told her, "Mom, the doctor says you need some help at home." She was fine with it, which surprised us. Then she said, "I want these two ladies." We asked, "What two ladies?" She explained, "Well, during my hospital stay I had a roommate who used two women for her home care. I met the two ladies who take care of her, and I want them to take care of me too." It turned out that these women worked independently, not for an agency. Not knowing anything about home care at the time, we didn't see that as a problem and my mom hired them to care for her. (In a later chapter you will see why their being "independent" should have raised a red flag.)

My mother passed in 2009. One of the caregivers came to the funeral, hugged all of our family, and told me how much she loved my mom. A few weeks later we discovered that this caregiver had been stealing from our mother. She was stealing from the very woman she cared for and professed to love! She wrote herself extra paychecks, and she was "cleaning out" the house. She took expensive items as well as inexpensive items (such as old tools and drinking glasses), likely to sell them off somewhere.

We were furious. How could she do such a thing? That incident drew my interest and attention onto home care. After my brother and I recovered from the shock of finding out that there are people base enough to steal from eighty-year-old women dying of cancer, many questions swirled around in our minds. Who are these people? How did this happen? Does it happen to others? What steps could we have taken to prevent this from happening?

Researching, I discovered that others have experienced this same sort of elder abuse. It's not prevalent, but it is definitely out there. And it's something most agencies don't talk about.

My brother and I approached the caregiver who stole, and she admitted to stealing $2,000. Well, thieves are also liars, and we knew it was much more than that. She agreed to pay at least the $2,000 back but never really did—just sent $100 here and there.

But the money wasn't the point. Even if she had paid back every penny, that wouldn't have sufficed. The deeper questions remain: How could she steal from someone she cared for? And how can we prevent this from happening to those we love? How can we use our experience to help other families avoid the same thing?

At that stage in my life I was ready to switch careers. Early in my career I had my own financial services firm. Since then I was an employee, working for others. Working for someone was never my ideal job. I wanted to be free to express my ideas and creativity. I wanted to set out and do my own thing again so I thought to myself, "I can do this! I can hire a better group of people. I can scare off the thieves and criminals, because I know what they're up to." I am no longer naïve. I know that just because someone calls themselves a caregiver does not mean they actually care.

Once I had the home care agency on my mind, examples of elder abuse seemed to pop up all around me. I began to see articles in the newspaper about so-and-so stealing from the elderly, about crime against the elderly being on the rise, etc. Browsing online, I would run across stories of people scamming seniors. The caregiver—be it a doctor, lawyer, nurse, aide, family member, etc.—took advantage of the trust they had been given. It is a problem but has mostly been the elephant in the room and not discussed.

I knew I had to get involved with this. Deep in my soul, I am really disgusted by people who take advantage of kids and who take advantage of the elderly. Pick on me, pick on you, pick on able-bodied person. But pick on the elderly? Those who stoop to that level are really the bottom of the barrel. By starting my own agency I knew I could offer a trustworthy alternative to those in need.

But before I could start the agency I had to figure out the business details. Sounds like fun, right? One option was to work for an established agency, one of the "big boys" here on the East Coast. That was no good. I looked at some franchise opportunities, but as an owner of a franchise it still feels like you are an employee since you answer to the franchisor and their corporate office. Try buying a McDonald's franchise and telling them, "Hey, you know what? We're not selling Quarter Pounders anymore, we're switching to hotdogs." That doesn't work. Plus, because they get a cut of your profits, the franchisors are constantly harassing you about the numbers. They tell you what to do and not to do, what to say and not to say. Nope, not for me. To me, that's not owning your own business—that's buying a job.

I opted to go the independent route and started Angel Alliance Caregivers from scratch. Setting out on my own gave me the freedom to do what I wanted to do. *Free* is not the same as *alone*: I received some great advice and mentoring along the way, and still do. But my hands aren't tied in any way, shape, or form.

Shortly before I started the agency I began to give seminars. The title of the seminar is *Broken Trust: Dealing with Elder Financial Abuse*. I still give that seminar regularly today. I share it with colleges, senior centers, hospitals, social worker groups, and anywhere else that will give me an ear. I explain who does this, why they do it, how they justify it, what to watch out for, and how to protect yourself and your loved ones. Every time I give a seminar, multiple people come up to me afterward to tell me that this has happened to a neighbor, a loved one or even themselves. Elder financial abuse is out there. I am grateful to be able to start the conversation on it.

When you walk into my office you will see a big corkboard with flyers for my seminar and newspaper articles posted all over it. It is right next to the table where we interview. I tell potential hires, "This is why I started this agency and I take this very seriously. If you steal or take advantage of a family while working for me, I will be sitting in court with the family."

I keep my agency a manageable size where I can oversee every employee. In addition, because of my personal experience, I let families know what to look for (and *look out* for) when considering home care. We feel our agency is better suited to protect you from those who would like to take advantage of you and your loved ones.

I have found that this approach scares away the bad people. Those who would do such things know who to work for and where to work and what to do—and working for me is a really bad place for them. Let's face it, bad people know bad people and good people know good people. I want the word to get around that I am the agency to work for if you are an honest caregiver. We are NOT the agency to work for if you are not. Many times these folks end up working under the table, advertising in the paper or on craigslist. That's what the woman who stole from our mom did; we understand she's still advertising herself as a home care aide on Craigslist and such. But she's not working for me! **And that is why I started this agency: to provide home care you can trust.**

Angel Alliance Caregivers serves two counties at the southern end of New Jersey: Atlantic County and Cape May County. We will likely expand to serve other counties in the near future. We're a non-medical health care service firm, licensed by the state of New Jersey. And New Jersey is a tough state when it comes to licensing: every year they check us out to make sure everything is still running properly.

Most of my business is helping seniors in need of companion care or providing what is called in New Jersey a Certified Home Health Aide. Here in New Jersey a companion can perform tasks such as meal preparation, light housekeeping, laundry, errands, and grocery shopping. They can make a sandwich, do the laundry, watch TV with the resident, make a run to the pharmacy, take the individual to the doctor, that sort of thing.

Once you get into any type of hands-on care you have to be a Certified Home Health Aide. That's when you are aiding folks who need hands-on help such as bathing, toileting, getting up from a chair, showering—really any physical contact. In order to perform that sort of care an aide has to be certified with the state of New Jersey. To get certified they must take a course, pass a background test, have a physical examination, and renew their license every two years. We provide both companion care and certified care to many clients.

One of the things that make us unique is that I am a very hands-on agency owner. When you call my agency, you will probably get ahold of me. I've opted not to use an answering service, so I answer the phones myself. I try to be very reachable. We have all wanted to talk with the boss before, whether of a plumbing company or cable company or some other company. It's nice to talk to the boss, but you rarely can. I cannot tell you how many times I have been on the phone and asked for a supervisor, but never gotten to the supervisor. Those employees are trained not to let you talk with a supervisor.

I want to know what is going on in the business at all times. Hiring a manager is always an option but managers tend to come and go. Home care has a high turnover rate. One day a manager is working at an agency, the next they're working for a nursing home, then at a hospital, and so on. It's the same with home health aides: high turnover. So it is very important to me that I know what is going on. If there is a problem, I want to know how I can help. I believe this allows the client to experience consistency. In addition no one is ever going to care more about a business more than the owner. No one. That is why I am very involved with my business. I always go over to the homes of new clients, to meet the family so they know what I'm all about. They get a feel for my personality and how I do things. That personal attention allows Angel Alliance Caregivers to stand out.

Angel Alliance Caregivers also stands apart from many other agencies in that we are a family-owned business. That's something I take pride in. My dad owned his own business, Thomas H. Banks and Associates. He had a great reputation and I want to have the same. In business, you can't buy a reputation. So here at Angel Alliance Caregivers we are building a really, really good reputation—one client at a time.

I hope you enjoy the book. May it help you select a trustworthy home care agency that will provide excellent care to your loved one for many years to come.

Greg Banks
September 2015

"What lies behind you
and what lies in front of you,
pales in comparison
to what lies inside of you. "
~ Ralph Waldo Emerson

There's No Place Like Home

Chapter 1: Signs Home Care is Needed

Americans are living longer today than ever before. According to the US Census Bureau, people age 65 and older will represent twenty percent of the population by the year 2030. That is nearly double the percentage of older adults living today!

While a longer life expectancy is most certainly something to be celebrated, a longer life is not without its own challenges.

According to the Alliance for Health Reform, 20 percent of seniors are living with five or more chronic conditions, seeing an average of 14 different physicians and using about 50 prescriptions every year.

These numbers are startling. One out of five older adults are living with chronic conditions such as Type II Diabetes, high blood pressure, high cholesterol, Alzheimer's disease, Parkinson's, and/or depression, etc.

As a result of aging, many older adults eventually require some level of care and assistance with daily living. Most find it challenging to ask for help. After all, people value their independence and privacy, and do not want to be a burden on their family and friends. We have learned that older adults, like all of us, want to continue living life to its fullest. In fact, their families, friends and health care professionals also want that for them.

There are telltale signs to look for that might indicate a need for outside assistance. Proactively addressing concerns can greatly facilitate a potential transition in lifestyle that ensures dignity and honor.

- Behavior/Demeanor - If your loved one appears more anxious or irritable about normal activities of daily living, this could be a sign that something is off kilter. Have previously outgoing parents become more introverted? Are important things being forgotten (taking medications, eating, personal hygiene, etc.)

- Hygiene/Cleanliness - Are you noticing that baths are becoming less frequent? Has she suffered a urinary tract infection? Are clothes, bed linens and towels laundered regularly? As you probably know, repeated shortcomings in this area can create even greater issues.

- Driving - Does your loved one's vehicle show signs of damage? Diminished hearing and/or vision can impair the ability to drive safely. Have there been incidents when your loved one has become disoriented or lost while going to a routine location?

- Medical Condition - Has there been a recent illness, injury or diagnosis? Clearly a new impairment can present new challenges and a need for assistance. Often, receiving an unexpected diagnosis can create psychological challenges and present a need for assistance.

- Medications - Are prescribed medications being taken properly? Are prescriptions being refilled on time? Is there a current list of all prescriptions? How are medications being monitored?

- Daily Tasks - The "routine" is important to monitor. Are meals being prepared or is this activity becoming too taxing? What about grocery shopping? Are baths avoided because of a fear of falling? Is basic household management routine, or has it become overwhelming?

- Mail/Finances - Is mail piling up? Are bills being paid? Are they able to appropriately manage their financial affairs? Are "junk mail" solicitations being accepted?

- Meals/Nutrition - Are you observing rapid weight gain or loss? This could indicate an unbalanced menu, missing meals altogether, or eating unhealthy alternatives. Are outdated or spoiled groceries still stocked in the refrigerator?

- Safety - Are home appliances turned off when not in use? Is the home free of unnecessary fall hazards? Are the doors and windows locked?

Concerns with even one of these issues may indicate that it is time to take a more active role in your loved one's life. Trust your instincts. Begin by sharing your concerns with your loved one in a respectful, non-threatening manner. Reinforce that your intent is to understand and respect his or her wishes while ensuring safety and comfort.

> *Beverly and Susan's Story*
> *Sisters Beverly and Susan requested a meeting because they were concerned about their mother's wellbeing. When we met, they described taking turns calling their mother every morning to ensure she had taken her medications and eaten. Since Beverly lived closer, she dropped by at least a couple of days a week to bring groceries and check on things. Susan did the laundry on her weekend visits with her mom.*
>
> *They discovered that, though their mother always assured them she had taken her medications and eaten, there were often untaken pills in the pill tray and spoiled food in the refrigerator.*
>
> *Fiercely independent, their mother refused to consider relocating to a nursing facility. Both daughters were committed to honoring their mother's wishes until Susan came down with a nasty case of the flu and Beverly had to go out of town for work.*
>
> *They soon realized that even the best-intentioned neighbors could not be relied upon for their mother's care. That is when they decided to explore home care options that would make all of their lives easier and empower their mother to remain in the comfort of her home.*

Often, there are simple things you can do to provide assistance with daily living. You may consider hiring a home care agency a few days a week. Choose an agency that offers care plans customized to your loved one's needs. Make certain the home care agency meets all state standards and that its caregivers are employees, who are thoroughly screened and appropriately trained and insured—not subcontractors.

Seek advice from a health care professional. To help you and your family feel more comfortable and confident in your caregiving decisions, consider joining a community support group and networking with other families who are dealing with similar issues.

Take the Path of Least Resistance

When first entertaining the idea of bringing help into your loved one's home, it may be wise to start with tasks that are non-threatening and less intrusive in regard to personal space. For instance, grocery shopping is a cumbersome task most would be greatly relieved to give up. As the agency performs this task, your loved one will get accustomed to someone coming and going from their home and providing help. Grocery shopping could lead to assistance with laundry or meal preparation. As a level of comfort is reached with each activity, other tasks can be added as needed.

Proactively observe for signs that home care might be needed. You do not want to be in a position of seeking assistance after the crisis or emergency.

There's No Place Like Home

Chapter 2: What IS Home Care?

Home care encompasses supportive services that empower people to continue living in their homes as independently for as long as possible. It involves assistance with essential activities of daily living. For the purpose of our discussion, this chapter addresses home care involving a professional, or paid, caregiver.

Home care generally falls into three categories:
1. Home health care
2. Hospice home care
3. Private duty home care

Our view is that home care—in all its varieties—should be designed to empower your loved one to regain or maintain as much independence as possible. With home health, that might mean help during recuperation from an illness or injury. With hospice, the goal might be to help your loved one finish his/her life's race with dignity and honor, as pain/symptom free as possible.

Private duty home care is oftentimes a stand-alone service. As an example, some caregivers may assist with bathing, dressing and meal preparation only, if there are no

other needs. However, if there are other needs, home care might very well be provided in conjunction with other supporting services like physical therapy or hospice. While we focus on private duty home care, it is also important to understand the services offered by both home health agencies and hospice organizations.

Home Health Care
Home health agencies may be licensed to provide care that includes skilled nursing care, and an aide for personal care, as well as physical, occupational, and speech therapies. Typically, their visits are short and specific in nature. It is common for both home health and home care services to be received over the same time period because the assistance provided is different.

If a hospital discharge planner arranges home health care for your loved one, do not make the mistake of assuming that assistance with all activities of daily living will be provided. A home health professional is with your loved one for an average of perhaps four to six hours out of the 168 hours in a week. For that reason, it is often suggested that home care services be provided in conjunction with home health services.

Hospice Care
Hospice care focuses on palliative (comfort) care for a terminally ill person. It provides pain and symptom management, and attends to emotional and spiritual needs, as well. Hospice home care includes regular scheduled visits by a registered nurse. Some hospice organizations have teams of volunteers who help with

respite care. Many choose to augment this care with the daily services a home care agency can provide.

Private Duty Home Care

This is supportive care that empowers a person to remain at home. It is known by many names - senior care, elder care, home care, and even sitter services. Sometimes, it is mistakenly referred to as "home health" although as a rule, home care does not include physical or occupational therapies.

Home care services can provide assistance and support in areas such as:
- Bathing and personal hygiene
- Transportation
- Meal preparation
- Light housekeeping
- Medication reminders
- Dressing and undressing
- Pet care
- Errands and grocery shopping
- Laundry and ironing
- Companionship and activities
- and much more.

We've heard professionals in home health describe home care as the "everything else folks." In other words, good private duty home care companies will structure services comprehensively, tailoring care plans to address needs beyond those met by skilled home health providers.

Home care services are beneficial in two primary categories—Recuperative Care and Continuing Care.

Recuperative Care
The goal of Recuperative Care is to empower the person to regain strength, confidence and stability in a safe environment. The caregiver might assist with transferring from the bed to a walker, for instance, or help with bathing or meal preparation. They might also encourage strengthening exercise "homework" given by an occupational or physical therapist. Just as a person may "graduate" from a wheelchair as he or she gets stronger, it is possible to improve to a point where home care services are no longer needed.

Continuing Care
In contrast, Continuing Care involves assistance with a long-term illness or injury. Like Recuperative Care, the services cover the range of issues listed above. The need for assistance may be due to anything from Alzheimer's or Parkinson's to stroke or mobility issues.

Licensing of Home Care Agencies
Roughly half of all states have licensing requirements. Some states only require a license if the agency serves Medicaid clients. If you are in a state that requires licensure, make certain that the agency chosen meets all requirements and holds the appropriate license.

Beyond licensing issues, it is also important to be comfortable with the degree of professionalism, experience and expertise of the serving agency. Be certain the agency conducts criminal background and national registry checks on their caregivers, that their employees are insured, bonded and covered by

Workers Compensation, and that they are experienced with your specific issues.

Having these foundational aspects in place is a necessary first step in ensuring proper care for your loved one. Now let's consider why Home Care may be your preferred choice.

There's No Place Like Home

Chapter 3: Why Is Home Care the Preferred Choice?

Most people prefer home care over any other option, and for good reason. They don't want to leave their homes! Wouldn't your loved one want to stay home if they could?

Home is a place of emotional and physical associations, memories and comfort. Leaving home is an emotional crisis that can be disruptive and result in some degree of depression. For some, assisted living facilities, retirement communities or nursing homes are the better option. They may find happiness in any of these facilities. But if at all possible, they are happiest if allowed to remain at home.

Home care offers everything from light housekeeping to skilled nursing. Because of this, people in all walks of life make it their first choice.

Consider the following ten reasons why home care is the most popular choice.

<u>10 Reasons for Home Care</u>

1. Independence — Who doesn't want independence? This is, perhaps, the greatest

advantage for receiving care in one's own home. It can be difficult to adjust to the regimented lifestyle of a facility, but at home you can set your own schedule, choose what and when to eat, and how and when to bathe. Even those with the greatest need for assistance report that home care empowers continued independence.

2. Family and Friends — Unlike the restricted visiting hours at hospitals and nursing facilities, home provides a place where family and friends can be close to the person at all hours, whenever needed. It isn't necessary to schedule a side room for Thanksgiving; you can sprawl out in your parent's home as you please. Nothing says "I've been institutionalized" like having to tell family and friends that visiting hours are limited to such and such hours. This isn't the case in your home.

3. Comfort — Being at home is simply more comfortable for most people than being in an unfamiliar place. At home, we have our photographs, books, bed, bath, kitchen, telephone, television and all the things we're accustomed to. Everything is in its place, which studies have proven to be an effective emotional healer. Even if you can take a few select items from home to a facility, and even if it is made as "home-like" as possible, it still cannot provide the comforts of your real home.

4. Faster Release from the Hospital — With home care, older adults might be able to go home

sooner from the hospital, since the services of nurses, doctors, therapists, social workers and caregivers can take place at home. This is great news for many people.

5. Faster Recovery — Research has shown that recovery can be faster at home than in the hospital, particularly if there is good quality, skilled home health care available. Many occupational therapists prefer home settings versus sterile hospital settings because that is where the normal activities of daily living take place. Faster recovery means a quicker return to normalcy.

6. Substitute for Hospital or Nursing Care — In some cases (depending on the severity of an illness or disability), home care can substitute for other forms of institutionalized care, including hospitals, skilled nursing homes and assisted living facilities. If a comprehensive individual care plan addresses every need, your home can be a perfectly suitable alternative.

7. Involvement with Treatment — Both the client and his or her family members can be more intimately involved with treatment at home. They can assist with medication administration, and physical therapy, and more effectively coach the patient on his/her continued recovery.

8. Morale — Patients tend to have a greater sense of well-being and higher morale when they are in the comfortable surroundings of their own home.

Dorothy had it right in The Wizard of Oz – "there's no place like home."

9. Promotes Healing — Older adults enjoy a better quality of life, which helps extend life, health & happiness. They are in a familiar environment, surrounded by family in both their home and community. This is particularly true with individuals living with Alzheimer's or other related dementia.

10. Cost — Depending on the services needed, home care can be much more affordable than a skilled nursing facility or other institutions.

Research indicates that "home" is the off-the-chart winner when people are asked where they want to age. The good news is that it can be a reality for most people.

Chapter 4: What is the Goal?

The goal of home care is to help people maintain and maximize their independence. Ideally, it should facilitate a person being able to remain as independent as possible for as long as possible in the setting of their choice—their home.

Clearly, independence can mean different things in different circumstances. To a person recovering from a hip replacement, independence might mean something entirely different from someone living in the early stages of Alzheimer's. No two situations are exactly the same, and while the degree of or nature of independence can vary widely, home care should be an empowering service.

Ms. Betty's Story
Betty, an active older woman, enjoyed playing Bridge with her friends and frequently held dinner parties in her home. She suffered a stroke, fell and injured her knee. After rehabilitation, Betty was unable to drive and was in no position to prepare for gatherings in her home. Home care services empowered her to continue participating in her favorite activities. In addition to personal care, she found value in other services including transportation and assistance around the home.

> *Oscar and Vera's Story*
> Oscar and Vera had lived in their home for over forty years. They could not imagine living anywhere else. Vera was in the middle stages of Alzheimer's and Oscar had mobility issues. A home care strategy was tailored that enabled them to continue living in their home. Personal care, meal preparation, housekeeping, transportation, and a host of other services were included in their care. Because of home care, they remained in their home safely and with every need fulfilled until Oscar's final breath. Though their basic needs would have been addressed in a skilled nursing facility, it is unlikely that this couple would have responded as well to the regimented lifestyle and loss of independence.

Beyond the person being served, home care should also be carefully tailored to empower family and friends of the person being served. Perhaps home care service enables family time to be quality time rather than time spent changing light bulbs and doing grocery shopping. Home care could provide the emotional relief that comes from knowing your parent is being cared for by professional and compassionate caregivers.

> *Katherine's Story*
> Katherine's family lived out-of-state. Their goal was to move her closer to them. In the months leading to that move, the family was empowered to be worry-free. Medical appointments were scheduled and transportation there and back was provided. Each

> day, a brief summary was written and emailed to family members. Within a week, her son responded with how thankful he was that he could focus on the impending move, free of anxiety about his mother's wellbeing.

Even when the basic needs of your loved one are addressed through home care, the service is not complete until you feel at ease with the arrangements. You'll recognize when you have received the highest quality home care when you no longer spend sleepless nights worrying about your parent's care.

Health care providers are better situated to provide the best care when they have, as Paul Harvey used to say, "the rest of the story." The best home care providers take daily care notes to document care. Doctors and psychologists report that having this documentation from a trained caregiver can be quite valuable.

> *Evelyn's Story*
> *We noted that Evelyn was showing significant memory issues over several weeks. The nearest adult child was out-of-state. Seeing our care notes, he requested we schedule an appointment with her family doctor. Her regular caregiver accompanied her to the appointment. When the doctor asked about the purpose of the visit, the patient could not remember. Had our caregiver not been there, she could easily have been given a quick look-over and sent home. Instead, the caregiver mentioned the patient's observed memory issues and the physician ordered a cognitive screening. In a very real sense, home care*

> *empowered this physician to fully address the needs of this woman.*

Home care is about empowerment.
Empowerment of the person being served.
Empowerment of family and friends.
Empowerment of health care professionals.

Rebecca's Story
We received a call from Rebecca, who was juggling many balls at once. She and her husband both worked full-time and were both engaged in volunteer activity. They had two boys, aged 12 and 14. One played soccer and another was in the Boy Scouts. Both enjoyed the playroom that had grown with them through the years. This was one busy family.

Rebecca was primarily interested in my experience with and thoughts about a few different assisted living facilities. I could tell she'd already made the decision to utilize one of them. I shared my thoughts on two I would recommend and another I could not. I asked how much her mother was involved in the selection and whether they had taken her to visit, and was shocked by Rebecca's response. She had never asked!

Rebecca assumed that her mother would never entertain the notion of living with her and that it would create such a major upheaval in her family's life that it just wasn't worth considering. I offered to meet with the family to provide an in-person review of the facilities she was exploring and to talk a little about some of the families we serve.

Like many of those we serve, Rebecca was eager to arrange a family meeting with everyone present. To Rebecca's surprise, her mother truly wanted to be invited into her daughter's home to live. And her sons were the ones to offer their playroom as their grandmother's bedroom.

As the wheels started turning in all of their minds, I shifted gears to start helping them navigate these waters. The new extended family unit felt fully empowered because they fully controlled every decision.

Rebecca expressed great relief that we were helping her mother and, though she made some adjustments in her activities, she felt like she had rebalanced her life to better reflect her values and beliefs. Because the boys had relinquished their playroom, they wanted to play a role in helping get their grandmother situated with her familiar furniture and decor. We involved everyone and even if tempers flared from time to time, everyone played a vital role.

During the transition period, we recommended an appointment with a respected geriatrician who became the new primary care physician.

In reviewing everyone's schedule and the various needs for assistance, we agreed on a service schedule that seemed to make everyone's life easier.

> *Rebecca's mother lived with them for almost three years before passing away. There were challenging times when Rebecca would second-guess her decision. However, I recently received a handwritten letter from her saying, "these were the best years of my life and, I think, my mother's too." She thanked us for providing the services and supports necessary to make it a reality. Though there was no way she could have known about this book, she thanked us for "empowering my family to do what we didn't think we could do. During difficult times, the Lord always sends angels to help along the way and that's what I think of when I think of [your company]."*

"Only those who will risk going too far
can possibly find out how far one can go."
~ T. S. Elliot

Chapter 5: At MY Home?

Once the need for assistance has been identified and accepted, the next question is, "Where?"

What is the most appropriate care setting?

As we've already noted, your loved one might prefer to remain at home. For some families, however, the next best option may be moving in with an adult son or daughter. While aging parents living with an adult child does require adjustment, the rewards tend to outweigh the challenges.

As we explore this option, we'll consider several issues.

Relationship and Arrangements

Have realistic expectations. As with any living arrangement, and particularly with every relationship, there are good days and bad days. The same will be true of having your parent live with you.

One of the first things you might consider is an honest assessment of your relationship with your parent. Do it from both your own and your parent's perspective. Do you share some of the same interests that could be cultivated in your home? Do you enjoy spending time together? Or, are there unresolved issues or grievances?

Also, consider having a talk and establishing a general understanding and even ground rules (e.g., is the parent going to contribute to expenses, participate in household activities/chore, will the parent have private quarters/bath, what about visitors, etc.).

Allow me to insert a word of caution here regarding less-than-stellar relationships. If you have not been close to your parent, do not expect that this new arrangement alone will create perfect harmony. In fact, it could very well exacerbate the situation.

It is often helpful to have a conversation (or series of conversations) with your parent with the goal of resolving past issues. Whether you were partially at fault, the victim, or a combination of both, don't bring a laundry list of grievances. Simply discuss the issues and offer a positive resolution that is mutually accepted.

Lastly, embrace the fact that not only is your parent your parent, he or she is also an individual. Likewise, you are not only their child, but are also an individual. Ideally, the relationship should be one of mutual respect. Your needs, likes and dislikes, and the way your home is run should be balanced with the desires of your parent. Express your feelings and wishes in a respectful way and listen (really listen) to your parent's feelings as well. The emotional support of simply listening can be as valuable as any financial or physical care provided.

The arrangements might be topsy-turvy for a while. That's okay. Expect it and embrace the change because the rewards can be tremendous.

Discuss the situation with any children who live at home. It is sometimes difficult for a child when another baby is brought into the family. The same could be true when you bring your parent home. The children may become jealous of attention paid to your parent. They don't always understand the reasons why their grandparent has moved in with them. Even worse, if their living space has been adjusted (for instance, a playroom converted into a bedroom for your parent), they might resent the new addition to the family.

Listen to and validate these potential emotions. Then explain, in as much detail as appropriate, the reasons why your parent has moved in. Be truthful, and use tact and age-appropriate language when communicating with children.

For example, if your parent is living with Alzheimer's, assure your child that it is not contagious, that your parent did nothing to get this disease, and the love and support from family can make a tremendous difference in regard to quality of life.

Bathroom
The bathroom can be the most dangerous room in your home. Take precautions to mitigate risks and ensure a safe and comfortable room.

See Chapter 12 for detailed information on bathroom safety.

Bedroom
A bedroom should be a place of sanctuary. Spend time together decorating your parent's bedroom to reflect their personality by including familiar items and décor, such as framed photos, flowers, mementos, and furniture. Avoid anything that would clutter, create fall hazards or make the room uninviting.

If mobility is an issue, ensure that a wheelchair or other assistive devices have plenty of room to enter and exit. It might be necessary to rearrange furniture or widen doorways. Always remind your loved one to tuck their elbows when passing through a doorway. Throw rugs are usually a bad idea, but if they are "a must," tape or otherwise secure them to the floor.

The bed should not be so tall that getting into it creates unnecessary drama or safety considerations. While sitting on the side of the bed, your parent's feet should touch the floor. Position the bed to provide access from both sides.

If incontinence is an issue, it might be appropriate to have a bedside toilet available. Store and position other assistive accoutrements to be readily available without causing the bedroom to feel cold and sterile.

Alzheimer's Disease

Is it feasible to move a parent who is living with Alzheimer's into your home? The answer largely depends on you. Having served many people living with Alzheimer's (or other related dementias) to their final breath in the comfort of their home, I can tell you that it is certainly possible. What I cannot tell you is whether you are prepared for the road ahead.

In the early stages, adjustments to your home will appear much different from the final stages. Invest in a label maker and a dry-erase board. In the early stages, consider labeling things to remind or orient your loved one about the contents within: drawers (silverware), cabinets (plates, towels, games, etc.), or closets, for example. Each morning, write the date, the day of the week, and any planned activity on the dry-erase board. Have picture and activity books or photo albums available. Explore known and previously undiscovered interests your parent might have and make those activities available (painting, container gardening, etc.). Involve your parent in meaningful activities like setting the table or folding laundry (even if you have to take the towel closet and dump it into a hamper for her to fold).

Resources are abundantly available to help you through the various stages of Alzheimer's. Home care agencies should be equipped to connect you to appropriate resources.

Again, you and your family and support network are the only ones who can determine if you should bring someone living with Alzheimer's into your home, but the resources, services and supports are available to make it a reality. Most families find that the emotional and other rewards can be tremendous.

"Hospital" Accessories

Some older adults require more extensive service and support. For example, your parent might require oxygen, have a G-tube (feeding tube) for nutrition, or use a Hoyer lift to get in and out of bed. Though use of this equipment might entail some brief training, it might not prevent you from caring for your loved one at home.

Mobility

Have a comprehensive environmental assessment conducted on your home by a trained professional. This will identify areas that need adjustment to accommodate special mobility issues.

Often, changes to accommodate mobility are minor. These changes might include shifting furniture so that a wheelchair or walker can freely maneuver, or removing throw rugs that create fall hazards. They might also include special attention to pets or children's toys.

Alternatives to Home Care

Home care may not be right for every situation. So let's review some alternatives to home care.

Skilled Nursing Facility

Nursing homes provide twenty-four hour care by trained staff. To accommodate staffing considerations and ensure efficient operation, your parent's days would be highly regimented with meals and activities occurring at specific times.

Depending on the factors that matter most to you when selecting a nursing home (e.g., location/convenience, reputation, cost, décor, staffing), it can be helpful to look at and compare multiple options. Take time to explore different facilities.

Questions to Ask in Determining Suitability:
- Do the staff members have "permanent assignments" or are they shifted from hall to hall? Permanent assignments allow your loved one to get to know their caregivers and build stronger relationships.
- Is the staff to resident ratio acceptable? What is staff turnover? Generally, the lower the turnover, the greater the continuity of care for your loved one.
- How flexible is the menu and meal schedule? Do they accommodate dietary restrictions based on culture or religion? Some facilities offer a flex-schedule for residents, giving them more choices.
- Ask family members of residents, what improvements they would most welcome? Ask if they've been happy with the facility. This may open the door for them to discuss any needed improvements or perceived problem areas.

Assisted Living Facility

While skilled nursing care is not provided as in a nursing home, there are some services available to help with activities of daily living. Meals are typically provided two or three times a day, medication reminders or administration given at appropriate times, and assistance with bathing might be available. Again, conduct careful research to ensure you choose the facility that best fits the needs and desires of your parent.

Independent Living Facility

Unlike skilled nursing or assisted living facilities, staff is not available to assist with activities of daily living or medical needs. In essence, this type of facility is a living arrangement for people of the same generation. There are usually planned group activities to promote socialization and provide entertainment. Often, there are shared resources available such as a laundry room, activities center, and gym.

What we've found is that many families go through a cycle of anxiety. The first stop in this trip is anxiety over not knowing what is available or where to even discover what's out there. Once they start to discover that there are many options, instead of easing the anxiety, it can actually exacerbate it.

You can mitigate some of the anxiety by talking with and listening to your parent regarding their wishes. Don't be surprised if their goal is to remain in their home.

There's No Place Like Home

"Anyone who keeps the ability to see beauty
never grows old"
~ Franz Kafka

There's No Place Like Home

Chapter 6: Planning for Discharge

Nancy's Story
A few years ago I received a call from Nancy, a schoolteacher. Clearly distressed, she was grasping for a life preserver. We had talked briefly several months previously about providing assistance for her mother, but because everything seemed to be going pretty well, she had not acted upon our discussions—that is, until her mother was hospitalized for a few days after a fall. And, previously unbeknownst to her, today was discharge day. Since the hospital was insistent that her mother leave, Nancy found herself facing an immediate crisis regarding her mother's ongoing care.

Fortunately, I was just blocks from the hospital when I took Nancy's call. After a quick U-turn, I met her mother and, because Nancy couldn't leave school at that time, I drove her mother home. While on our way, I contacted my office to arrange for a caregiver to meet us at the home.

What was nearly a discharge catastrophe ended up okay, but it was only the result of happenstance rather than planning.

Jim's Story
Contrast that story with that of Jim and his father. When Jim first contacted me, his father, who had been undergoing rehabilitation, was scheduled for discharge in a week. Because Jim planned ahead, we had ample time to meet his father, assess the situation, and choose just the right caregiver. The staff at the

> *rehabilitation facility were thrilled that Jim's father would be discharged virtually worry-free; everything had been taken care of days prior to his leaving the facility.*

It is easy to get overwhelmed when a loved one is admitted to the hospital or a rehabilitation facility. Where is the road leading? What's next? Who can help me navigate these waters?

It will make your life easier if you start planning for discharge at the time of admission! Here are a few tips to make this planning easier and to empower your loved one to return home safely.

Who

There are a few key people you should meet and become familiar with soon after admission. Good communication with these people can go a long way toward making discharge as worry-free as possible.

One of the most important people to meet is the case manager since his or her job is to help facilitate discharge. The case manager, usually a social worker or nurse, could be assigned to your loved one's floor or unit, or found in the case management office in the facility.

Since case managers coordinate discharges and other issues for many patients, their workload can be daunting. Approach them with consideration and respect because a good relationship helps ensure good communication at the time of discharge.

The attending physician and nursing staff are important for many of the same reasons. Let them know of your concerns for your loved one. They provide important information that can prove invaluable at the time of discharge

What and Where
It is not the time to be timid when discussing your desires for discharge. If it is your choice, clearly share your intention to return the patient to the comfort and care of home, thus providing the case manager with a specific direction in determining the direct actions that will ensure a smooth transition.

Have an idea of what you want to happen at discharge. Will your mother return to her home or go to a skilled nursing facility? Do you already have a relationship with a home care agency? If not, do you know someone who could make a recommendation? Be as specific as possible with the case manager and make sure he or she knows your and your loved one's desire for discharge.

Unfortunately, it sometimes seems the path of least resistance for a case manager is to discharge to a skilled nursing facility. Often hospitals have relationships with these long-term care facilities and doctors have admitting authority. However, if home is the desired location, make sure the case manager is working toward that goal.

If a return home is the plan, there are very likely other issues to address—mobility and accessibility considerations (ramp, grab bars, etc.), wheelchair or walker, emergency medical alert, home health services, home care services, etc.

When
The time to start thinking about and planning for discharge is at or shortly after admission.

- Meet the attending staff - physician(s), nurses, aides and case manager.
- Depending on the prognosis, start planning for discharge home and share this goal with the case manager.
- Make certain the case manager is aware of your preferred home service providers. If you don't have preferences, the case manager may offer recommendations. If so, check them out on your own to ensure a comfort level.
- Talk to service providers (Home Health, private duty home care, hospice, home medical equipment, etc.)
    - Get a tentative service schedule post-discharge (e.g., How often will the physical or occupational therapists visit?).
    - Ensure needed supplies and equipment are delivered (e.g., wheelchair, adult briefs, oxygen, etc.).
    - Meet the home caregiver and offer to show them around the home.
- Talk to family, friends and others who will be active in providing care/support.
- Verify transportation home.

- Stock the home with groceries, supplies and other sundries before discharge. *
- Turn on the air/heat, change the bed linens and neaten up the home. *
- Verify the supply of existing prescriptions and get refills of anything needed.
- Pick up any new prescriptions.

* Your home care agency can often handle these responsibilities prior to discharge.

How

Find out what accoutrements will be needed at home. Convey any preferences for equipment, pharmacies or services to the case manager beforehand. Certain items (like a wheelchair) are covered through Medicare. Some (like grab bars for the bathtub) are not.

Your home care agency should conduct an assessment of the living environment prior to discharge. A good agency will have the experience and expertise to discuss and make recommendations. A better agency will also be able to offer referrals to appropriate resources (someone who might do bathroom renovations to improve accessibility, for instance).

The home care agency assessment is actually two-fold. Not only will they visit the home environment, but they will also assess the patient at the hospital or facility. This is to ensure a safe, effective transition home.

There's No Place Like Home

Chapter 7: What Questions to Ask

If the decision is that your loved one will return home with the support of home care services, it's time to examine some specific questions for private duty home care companies. So where do you go now?

Choosing the right home care company can be a daunting challenge. Whom can you trust? What company will provide the best care, and treat your loved one with dignity and respect?

Many people who come to us are burning the candle at both ends as they worry about a parent. The company or agency you select to provide care should not add to the worries, but rather give you relief, assurance and confidence.

10 Vital Signs
Consider these ten questions when selecting a home care provider for a loved one. I refer to them as vital signs of a healthy company.

1. What is the company's background? Do a little research and check out the company and their history. Find out who owns the company and look at their experience and background. Is the company reputable and in good standing? Is the management involved in professional organizations? What do others who have experience with them have to say? You can find a lot online and it's definitely better to know

about the agency on the front end, before any commitment has been made.

2. How long has the company been in business? The number of years an agency has been in business is not always directly related to the quality of care given, but it does reflect upon the stability and success of the company. An experienced agency will be more likely to have support and supervisory staff and a team of caregivers sufficient to prevent missed days of service.

3. Is their staff of caregivers made up of employees or contract workers? Your preference should be that the agency employs the caregivers assigned to your parent. If you have stumbled upon an agency that employs contractors as caregivers, you might have problems. Ask about your personal liability and tax obligations if the agency's caregivers are contract employees. You can unknowingly accept substantial responsibility if you choose an independent contractor (federal and state payroll taxes, Workers Compensation, etc.). Be safe and stick with agencies whose caregivers are their employees.

4. Are their caregivers insured and bonded? For your protection, ensure that all caregivers are insured and bonded by the home care agency. If transportation of your loved one is involved, make sure the company is insured to provide this service as well. This protects you, the caregiver

and the agency in the event that something happens. Guess who is liable if they are not insured or bonded? You guessed it—you.

5. How do they supervise their workers to make sure proper care is given? Some agencies make scheduled quality assurance calls and visits. To further ensure quality care, see that all caregivers are regularly and closely supervised by qualified management. How are time records kept? If grocery shopping or other errands are required, how are those expenses addressed? Many agencies have automated clock in/out procedures and others ask that you sign time sheets. It's important to have open lines of communication with supervisory staff to ensure that evolving needs are met to your satisfaction.

6. Will the same caregiver be with my loved one on each visit? It is difficult to receive good care if different people show up every week. A good home care provider will be concerned with continuity of care. If the arrangement described involves a stranger going out to help a stranger in a strange home, run. You may want to meet the assigned caregiver prior to service commencement to ensure a good match. Even so, "life happens" from time to time and your regular caregiver might be unable to work on a particular day. How will the substitute be introduced and properly briefed on your loved one's care?

7. Do they conduct an in-home consultation and what does that include? When choosing the home care services that are right for you, it is important that the client and family members discuss the kind of care needed with an experienced home care professional. The assessment should include physical, cognitive, environmental (the home), and other areas of concern. The assessment provides a valuable opportunity for you to assess the professionalism of the company and gives the agency pertinent information from which to tailor a care plan.

8. Can they coordinate other types of services and supports? Is the company familiar with other services and able to make referrals or arrange for home accessibility companies, meals on wheels, medical alerts, geriatrician recommendations, etc.? As opposed to a phone book or trying to navigate uncharted waters on your own, the agency should be able to guide you to appropriate resources.

9. Can they provide testimonials from clients and their families?

10. Do they guarantee customer satisfaction? Find out if there is a length of time you will be committed to the home care provider even if you are unhappy with the care they provide.

The answers to these questions should give you some confidence. If they don't, check out another agency. If you are not comfortable with the arrangement (even if your parent's needs are met) and find yourself calling to check on their wellbeing throughout the day, the service can improve. The agency should not only be able to take care of your parent--they should do it in such a way that puts your mind at ease.

In answering these questions about my company, I'm pleased to say that we meet or exceed every standard. In fact, we're passionate about providing the highest quality of care that results in the highest quality of life. Our goal is empowerment and we believe meeting these standards is necessary in achieving that goal.

Jennifer and Dorothy's Story
My jaw dropped when I first met Jennifer and her mother, Dorothy. As we sat in Dorothy's living room, she was slumped back on the couch. They were looking to replace another agency with which neither of them was pleased. Their questions to me were directed to the issue of caregiver screening and supervision. As they developed a little trust with me, Jennifer shared that she had temporarily moved in with her mother because every morning before her caregiver arrived, Dorothy would cry and plead that she could make it on her own without any help.

The issue was that the present agency simply provided poor care with untrained and ill-suited staff, who were largely unsupervised.

We immediately commenced services. After only a few weeks of service, we received the following from Jennifer:

> "Only God could have assembled this team for my mom. In the midst of all that is going on it is a constant reminder that He loves us and we are blessed. Thank you for being the person He used to bring the team together. We are all sharing some sweet times together."
>
> I don't think it was because there was anything miraculous in what we did. Very simply, EVERY agency should hold itself to similarly high standards, though sadly they do not. To the degree practical, make sure the agency you select meets YOUR high standards.

"The only rock I know that stays steady, the only institution I know that works is the family."
~ Lee Iacocca

Chapter 8: The Risks in Hiring Through a "Caregiver Registry"

Families go through common cycles as they first navigate the waters seeking appropriate home care for a loved one. Having counseled countless families on these issues, we know the pitfalls and traps.

The Traps

First, the responsible family member(s) might be anxious about finding the right home care option. Some do not even know that such services exist. Others are unsure of how to go about arranging services. Once a few phone calls are made and information is received, you can easily reach information overload—the second stop in the cycle.

Cutting through the clutter is not always easy and sometimes the differentiator appears to be cost.
There are many home care agencies. The challenge begins in choosing the right one. Not all agencies are equal, and not all maintain their caregivers as employees.

Hiring an agency or company that utilizes independent contractors can be attractive. The cost could be as much as $5 less per hour—which translates into big savings over the long haul. Yet, it is important to understand the pitfalls of hiring an independent contractor rather than an employee caregiver.

While a family must stay within budgetary constraints, cost is only one consideration. When cost is the primary concern, families are tempted to "hire" an independent contractor or retain the services of a company whose caregivers are independent contractors. They do so at their own peril.

Employee-Employer Relationships

Sadly—though commonly—caregivers who are independent contractors might not realize the implications of working directly for a client. An employer/employee relationship has been established when the client outlines a service schedule and work required and the contractor agrees to it.

Often referring caregiver registries or independent contractor companies do not share with their client that he/she has assumed an employer/employee relationship with the independent contractor caregiver. Because of this, both the worker and the vulnerable older adult can suffer significant financial liabilities.

Payroll Taxes

When a worker receives a paycheck, he/she must pay appropriate taxes, including Social Security, Medicare, both state and federal unemployment, and both state and federal payroll taxes.

As the employer, the consumer (the person in need of care) is responsible for compliance. The government could sue the consumer (or their estate) for back taxes, including interest and penalties. When this situation has existed for many months or years, the tax responsibility could be substantial. Beyond simply collecting back taxes, interest and penalties, the government could also pursue civil and criminal penalties.

The situation is no brighter for the worker. With no payment into Social Security, they could become financially vulnerable in older age.

Workers Compensation Versus Home Owners Insurance

Employers are mandated to provide Workers Compensation coverage for their employees. If the worker sustains an injury on the job, liabilities can be substantial for the employer—this could be you if you have an independent contractor in your home. Since many home insurance policies specifically exclude employees in the home, any incurred medical costs or disability payments would be borne by the client. This could cause significant financial hardships for even the wealthiest employers.

The Horror Stories

We would hope that anyone who offers to care for an aging person in need of personal care or assistance is cut from the highest moral fabric. Unfortunately, this is not always the case. There are those who prey upon vulnerable people, taking advantage—financially and sometimes physically—of people to whom care is provided. (See the Preface for my personal story.) For this type of cruel person, it is all too easy to mistreat, abuse or otherwise harm a cognitively impaired or physically challenged person. Again, this could subject the person in need of care to physical or psychological abuse and financial exploitation.

The danger is real. Protections are not in place with independent contractors since they are not subjected to the hiring processes of a company or agency. It's likely they haven't had criminal background or national registry checks performed, successfully passed drug screening, or even had past employment history verified. This puts unsuspecting, often desperate, patients in jeopardy.

Supervision
Internal Revenue Service regulations clearly stipulate that independent contractor agencies cannot provide any substantive work supervision, scheduling or training to their workers. If they do, the relationship becomes an employer/employee relationship between the caregiver and their sponsoring agency.

Supervision, training and scheduling can only take place by companies or agencies that hire their workers as employees. When a client hires a caregiver directly, they are now responsible for all those considerations.

The Bottom Line
If you are considering hiring an independent contractor to provide care for an aging loved one, only do so if

you are also interested in becoming an employer and assuming all of the associated responsibilities.

If you hire an independent contractor to perform personal care for a loved one, YOU have just become the employer. As the employer, you are responsible for:
- Workers Compensation
- Federal and State payroll taxes
- Scheduling (including replacements or fill-ins)
- Supervision

Other important considerations that you would assume could include:
- Drug screening
- Background checks
- Past employment verification
- Professional Liability Insurance
- Bonding
- Training (could include CPR, First Aid, CNA)

Hire an independent contractor, if you must. But do so at your own peril.

There's No Place Like Home

Chapter 9: Geriatric Care Managers

From time to time, someone (usually from out of state) asks about Geriatric Care Management. They may not use those very words, but the underlying questions typically fall into a few familiar categories. Is it safe for mom/dad to remain in their home, and what can we do to make it safe? What living and/or care arrangements would we recommend?

Without a doubt, the leading reason families call is concern.

Perhaps a parent is in declining health or is unable to perform basic activities of daily living safely. Perhaps some incident has abruptly changed the situation, such as a fall, injury or illness. Whatever the case, the family is concerned and is seeking assistance with his or her parent.

Occasionally, there is concern that a parent has become un-engaged in previously enjoyed activities, such as attending church gatherings or family outings. In such cases, the concern is for a continued standard and quality of living. The objective is to maintain or regain the highest quality of life possible.

Some private home care companies provide geriatric care services that address these issues at no or nominal additional charge. You might also consider hiring a professional Geriatric Care Manager.

Fee structures vary widely when you hire a Geriatric Care Manager. Frequently, there is an initial assessment that could range from $200 to $500. This is a comprehensive evaluation of all aspects of the situation, including physical and mental health, environmental considerations, support networks, etc. From information gathered, an initial Care Plan is drafted. Typical hourly rates might range from $100 to $200 per hour and could be segmented into portions of an hour. The fees are largely dependent on the experience and expertise of the Geriatric Care Manager and the specific scope of service.

In some cases, Long-Term Care insurance policies cover some or all of the expense associated with Geriatric Care Management. Check the fine print and consult your claims representative to determine coverage.

So what do Geriatric Care Managers do? What is their value? The most skilled Geriatric Care Managers carefully assess each case, finding the "big picture," including all aspects of your parent's life, and individual situation (physical, cognitive and emotional). Based on the information gathered, they draft a comprehensive Care Plan addressing all concerns. This plan of care provides the specific road to a greater quality of life. It is the foundation from which they coordinate and supervise proper execution of the plan.

A good Geriatric Care Manager coordinates service to meet a host of concerns:
- Make recommendations with regard to the best living arrangements
- Facilitate growing old in their own home (far and away the preference of most older adults)
- Advise on options:
  - Independent or Assisted Living Facilities
  - Skilled Nursing Facilities
  - Special Care Units
  - Ramps or home access or safety considerations
- Schedule and accompany to medical appointments
- Coordinate private duty homecare assistance with day-to-day activities:
  - Bathing and personal hygiene
  - Meal preparation
  - Transferring
  - Dressing, feeding and other home care needs
- Coordinate transportation to visit friends or to appointments
- Arrange grocery shopping
- Provide medication reminders
- Arrange cognitive screening or tests
- Arrange for pet care
- Organize the household
- Pick up prescriptions
- And much more…

A good Geriatric Care Manager analyzes the situation and offers their best advice for the road ahead. This service can be invaluable to family members in search of timely and relevant guidance.

What should you look for in a Geriatric Care Manager?

First and foremost, the manager should have a passion for serving older adults. Clearly, you should want service from someone with experience and expertise. If someone calls herself a Geriatric Care Manager but does not have documented and verifiable experience and expertise, steer clear. What you should look for is someone trained in and expert with conducting assessments, who can transition into the role of manager to coordinate needed services and supports. Just as you want your auto mechanic to know every intricate detail about your car to ensure its optimum performance, you should seek the same with a Geriatric Care Manager.

The Bottom Line

If you believe you need the assistance of a Geriatric Care Manager, you might consider discussing your concerns with a private duty home care provider first. It is possible that they could conduct a no-obligation, comprehensive assessment free of charge, and, if there is a need for home care, they should be able to help. If not, they should be able to present a plan with options so that you can make the most informed decision regarding care for your loved one.

Chapter 10: Pride, Independence and Money

We've all heard it—"I don't need any help" or "I don't want a stranger in my home." Even when everybody involved believes assistance is needed, sometimes it is simply rejected. Why?

After talking to hundreds of families and assessing a variety of situations, I believe there are only a few reasons why someone in need of assistance rejects it—Pride, Loss of Independence, and/or Money.

<u>Pride</u>

Many older adults have grown up being self-sufficient and are known for "pulling themselves up by their boot straps." Pride can result in those with hearing impairments refusing to consider hearing aids; those who walk unsteadily refusing to use a cane or walker, and the list goes on. Many simply don't want to appear "old."

Sometimes the refusal has less to do with the type of assistance and more to do with who is providing it. There are some things we can do that a family member just can't. Perhaps it's something they feel uncomfortable doing. For instance, I would not relish the thought of one of my sons bathing me or changing my briefs, but one of our trained and experienced caregivers can assist in such a way as to preserve dignity and honor without the emotional discomfort.

I've found that it is more helpful to focus on the benefits of assistance rather than on the loved one's deficit(s). For example, that hearing impaired person might enjoy the benefit of hearing a granddaughter's piano recital, or the unsteady one might appreciate the benefit of making it onto the sidelines of a grandson's soccer game. While respecting the older adult's pride, focus on the benefits and empowerment achieved through such services or supports.

One of the most important aspects of our service is ensuring the right match. When the right caregiver with the right experience and the right training and, perhaps most importantly, the right personality is matched with a client, the outcomes can be tremendous. Not only can life be added to each day, but also I firmly believe that days can be added to life.

Independence

Outside of NASCAR enthusiasts, "taking the keys away" is less about driving and more about the loss of independence. The thought of losing one's independence is frightening, whether we're talking about the inability to drive safely, to make it to the toilet on time or any number of other limitations an older person faces. Besides this, many older adults have witnessed their peers' loss of independence, and that does not conjure happy thoughts.

Facing these issues, services and supports should be tailored to empower continued independence, or as much independence as is possible under the circumstances.

> **Ms. Smith's story**
> Ms. Smith suffered a stroke, had a fall, and was no longer able to drive. Frankly, nothing bothered her more than fighting traffic and, even before the stroke, she was aware that her driving skills had suffered. Even so, she enjoyed getting out and especially liked entertaining. Home care services provided transportation for her regular appointments (including numerous social outings), housekeeping and helping her get ready for dinner parties. Private duty home care empowered her to retain as much independence as possible and maintain her quality of life. She actually admitted how much easier it was now that she had help.

Sometimes it is not as much about "what" service is provided as how it is described. Words matter. Instead of describing a service as "full assist with bath," consider saying something along the lines of, "we'll help to make your bath safe so that you're refreshed and ready for the day."

Always respect an older adult's dignity and pride. When there is an expressed concern about loss of independence, go out of your way to assure your loved one that their independence is important to you. Explain that your intent is to empower their continued independence by helping out in a few areas.

Money

Mrs. Walker's story
Several years ago we were asked to provide care for Mr. Walker's wife who was living in the advanced stages of Alzheimer's. Mr. Walker explained that his biggest concern was in Mrs. Walker's personal hygiene. Though he was very helpful in other areas of her life, he did not feel comfortable in keeping his wife clean.

Because of the hourly rate we charged, Mr. Walker requested an exceptionally small service schedule. This family had done well financially and had the resources to secure needed services, but Mr. Walker could not get past the notion of actually paying for the service.

Within a two-hour service period scheduled three times each week, Mr. Walker wanted us to wash and change the bed linens (which his wife would sleep in soiled between visits), bathe his wife (who would go without bathing between visits), and clean up accidents that would have gone unattended between visits.

His desire was for his wife and home to be clean and safe, and that they'd be able to remain in the familiar surroundings of their home. There was a drastic disconnect between what he wanted and what could reasonably be provided within his budget.

I often think of this experience when counseling families with the resources but not the willingness to pay for services. While I can certainly understand and respect

> *living within one's means, I cannot understand having the financial resources and denying care.*

Money, or the lack thereof, can be a very real impediment to receiving needed services. People in need of home care services and supports typically fall into three groups relative to money: those who have the resources to pay for services, those who do not, and those who are on the line.

Those who have very little income or assets might qualify for Medicaid benefits. Those who are on the line can present a challenge. They could possibly qualify for assistance from the VA (Aid & Attendance), grants, or possibly even consider a reverse mortgage in some cases.

The first group has the financial resources to pay for services if they come to recognize the need. However, the ability to pay for services does not necessarily result in quality service.

This group of people might have a concern about outliving their savings, so they try to hold onto as much of it as possible. Though this is a valid concern, it should not result in cutting corners with regard to care. Care Plans must be structured to ensure flexibility, and carefully tailored to respect budgets while meeting the most pressing needs.

One pitfall we routinely see is with families seeking assistance from independent contractors. The "sticker price" of an independent contractor might be as much as $5 less per hour than a reputable provider. It's what they might not consider that can open them up for substantial liability and risk.

For more information on Independent Contractors, see Chapter 8 and the Preface.

Chapter 11: Fall Prevention Tips

Many older adults have an emergency medical alert that provides assistance at the touch of a button 24 hours a day, seven days a week. However, taking proper precautions beforehand could mean you never have to touch that button!

We've spoken thus far to family members. With Fall Prevention in mind, we want to share the following information directly with seniors concerned about falling.

Keep moving
Physical activity can go a long way toward fall prevention. Speak with your doctor about activities such as walking, water aerobics or Tai Chi. Such activities reduce the risk of falls by improving strength, balance, coordination and flexibility.

Tell the doctor if you fear physical activity will make a fall more likely. The doctor may recommend carefully monitored exercise programs or refer you to a physical therapist. A physical therapist can create a custom exercise program aimed at improving balance, flexibility, muscle strength and gait.

Wear sensible shoes
Consider changing your footwear as part of your fall-prevention plan. High heels, floppy slippers and shoes with slick soles can make you slip, stumble and fall, as can walking in your stocking feet.

Instead:
- Have your feet measured each time you buy shoes, since foot size can change.
- Buy properly fitting, sturdy shoes with nonskid soles.
- Avoid shoes with extra-thick soles.
- Choose lace-up shoes instead of slip-ons, and keep the laces tied. If you have trouble tying laces, select footwear with fabric fasteners.

Remove home hazards

Inspect your home for fall hazards. The living room, kitchen, bedroom, bathroom, hallways and stairways are common areas for hazards.

To make your home safer:
- Remove boxes, newspapers, electrical cords and phone cords from walkways. Keep main corridors free of clutter.
- Move coffee tables, magazine racks and plant stands from high-traffic areas.
- Secure loose rugs with double-faced tape, tacks or a slip-resistant backing—or remove loose rugs from your home.
- Repair loose, wooden floorboards and carpeting right away.
- Store clothing, dishes, food and other necessities within easy reach.
- Immediately clean spilled liquids, grease or food.
- Use nonskid floor wax.
- Use nonslip mats in your bathtub or shower.

Light up your living space
Keep your home brightly lit to avoid tripping on objects that are hard to see.

- Place night lights in your bedroom, bathroom and hallways.
- Place a lamp within reach of your bed for middle-of-the-night needs.
- Make clear paths to all light switches.
- Turn on the lights before going up or down stairs.
- Store flashlights in easy-to-find places in case of power outages.
- Consider trading traditional switches for glow-in-the-dark or illuminated switches.

Use assistive devices
Your doctor might recommend using a cane or walker to keep you steady. Other assistive devices can help, too.

For example:
- Hand rails for both sides of stairways
- Non-slip treads for wood steps
- A raised toilet seat or one with armrests
- Grab bars for the shower or tub
- A sturdy plastic seat for the shower or tub—plus a hand-held shower nozzle for bathing while sitting down

Putting these precautions in place will not guarantee against accidents, but it will reduce the incidence of them.

There's No Place Like Home

Chapter 12: Bathrooms Can Be Dangerous

The bathroom can be the most dangerous room in your home, but your home care provider should be able to offer recommendations for making it safer. By making the bathroom safer and creating a more inviting space, you can empower older adults to meet personal hygiene concerns and reduce dangers and fears.

According to the Centers for Disease Control and Prevention, every year almost a quarter of a million people visit emergency rooms because of injuries suffered in the bathroom, and almost 14 percent of those are hospitalized. Research has found that injuries increase with age, peaking after 85. People over 85 suffer more than half of their injuries near the toilet.

Fear is a common reason that personal hygiene begins to suffer. Put simply, your loved one might be scared to get in the bathtub because he or she has heard of others who have fallen in the bathroom. Getting into and out of a tub can be frightening to someone becoming unsteady. Because of this, your loved one may have decided to skip a bath altogether. Likewise, it's realistic to expect accidents when getting onto and up from the toilet is a challenge.

Here are some helpful tips in preventing bathroom accidents:

- Bathroom door - The door needs to be at least 32 inches wide, especially if the person you're caring for uses a walker or wheelchair, (If you're doing a bathroom remodel, you might consider widening the doorway whether you're loved one uses a wheelchair or not. You don't know what the future will bring.)
- Doorknob - A conventional doorknob can be difficult for older adults with arthritis or poor hand strength to grasp and turn. If so, replace the knob with a lever or push-button device for easy opening.
- Bathroom floor - The floor should have a nonslip surface, as should standing areas in the bathtub or shower. Remove throw rugs or place anti-slip mats under them.
- Lock - Install a lock that can be opened from the outside even while locked from the inside. If a person falls or becomes unconscious while inside a locked bathroom, you need to get in quickly.
- Walk-in tub or shower - A walk-in tub or shower enables an older adult to step directly in rather than up, over, and down.
- Grab bars - Put easily accessible grab bars in the tub or shower. Grab bars should be able to support a person's weight and should have a circumference of 1.5 inches. Allow about 2

inches between the grab bar and the shower wall.
- Handheld showerhead – These make it easier to direct water where it's needed.
- Taps - The hot- and cold-water controls should have easy-turn levers and be easy to reach while outside the tub.
- Shower shelves - Soap, shampoo, and towel should be easily reachable while sitting in the tub. Shelves that hold shampoos and soaps in the shower should be at chest height and conveniently close to avoid stooping and stretching.
- Counter space - There needs to be plenty of counter space to hold medicines, supplements, and personal toiletries.
- Corners - Counter edges around the sink should be rounded, not sharp.
- Grab bar - The toilet should have a grab bar on either side to help get up and down.
- Toilet roll - Should be able to reach the toilet paper easily.
- Room to roll - If a walker or a wheelchair is in use, you'll need plenty of free floor space around the toilet: 32 to 42 inches on the side and 18 inches in front.

By addressing these concerns, you will create a welcoming space that can safely accommodate your loved one's bathroom needs.

There's No Place Like Home

Chapter 13: Family Dynamics

Over the years, we have served and counseled countless families. While no two situations are exactly the same, there are a few constants. I believe it makes people more comfortable to know they are not alone and their situation is actually more common that they might believe.

A quick note to the only child: don't worry. We understand the burden of bearing complete responsibility for care of a loved one who needs assistance. Siblings can supply relief and support. However, an only child (or a child whose siblings live far away) can get that relief and support from home care services.

Actually, in virtually every family there is one adult child who, for whatever reason, is the one with the overall responsibility. This is true whether there are ten adult children or only...one.

A benefit of being an only child is that you do not have to deal with the Pigeons, Bears or Turtles that others do. Let me explain.

Pigeons

In some families, we see pigeons. The scenario involves a client with both a local adult child and one or more who do not live locally. You know you have a pigeon as a sibling if

they swoop into town, second-guess every decision you've made, and every action you've taken, issue proclamations about the way things should be handled, and then fly back home. In short, pigeons come and leave what pigeons do on the ground. Then, just like pigeons, they fly away with little concern over the mess they've created.

Pigeons want to feel as though they are involved in the care of their parent, even if they aren't (and have made no effort to do so). Before a pigeon arrives, make sure you can justify - even though you should not have to - decisions made and actions taken on your parent's behalf. It could save you some heartache. If possible, arrange a meeting with your home care provider to review your parent's Care Plan with your pigeon sibling(s). Sometimes when it comes from a third party, an outside expert, the decisions can be substantiated without causing hard feelings. We call these meetings, "taming the pigeon."

In any event, know in advance that you will be second-guessed and potentially undermined. Take refuge in the fact that you are doing the best you can under the circumstances, and that if your sibling wanted to play a more active role you would gladly accept their assistance.

In the end, the pigeon will leave you to clean up the mess, so, to the degree possible, minimize the mess.

There's No Place Like Home

Bears

The second type of sibling is a bear. For bears, it is perpetually wintertime and they will do what bears do - hibernate. These are the ones who, whether local or not, cannot accept the situation. They are in denial, sometimes in spite of overwhelming evidence that refutes their position.

> *Shirley the Bear's story*
> *A bear we dealt with was certain that her mother should continue driving even with her "declining memory." Her mother was living with advanced stage Alzheimer's disease. We found it necessary to remind this particular bear of the state of her mother's home before we started service: yard clippers were found with dinner plates in the pantry, dirty dishes were stacked in the oven, trash was found in the washing machine, and that was just the kitchen!*

The best you can hope for with bears is that they come around at their own pace to accept the reality of the situation. Though they seem to have an answer for everything, their answers may be a psychological protection against facing reality.

Tread lightly with bears who are living in denial. As with the actual animal, bears can react fiercely and in anger. Be honest with them about diagnoses, prognoses and the entire situation, but do so in a patient and respectful manner. Denial is

a powerful emotion and overcoming it takes patience and understanding.

Turtles

Another family member we see is the turtle. You might have guessed it, but turtles are slow moving. They are slow in recognizing a need for assistance, and sometimes slower in acting on the need.

Turtles want a complete road map, including hotels to stay in and sights to see on their summer vacation next year. They want to know where the road is leading and what is around the bend.

Certainly it would be helpful to know how care for an aging parent will evolve over time. Even so, at some point, you must take action. Turtles are averse to that. Sometimes they drag their feet so long that the crisis becomes even more severe.

If you have a turtle sibling, you must emphasize the need for a proactive approach to avoid potential pitfalls. Your home care provider might be able to reassure turtles by sharing their experience regarding families in similar situations.

Every family and every situation has its peculiarities and special considerations. Yet quite a few families we've served have had at least one pigeon, bear or turtle. If your family doesn't, you are most fortunate!

Chapter 14: How to Take Those Keys

When should I take the keys from my parent? This is one of our most frequently asked questions. Because of that, we've been involved in many family discussions over the years.

There are several reasons why someone should not drive. While not directly attributable to age, older adults might be more prone to these conditions.

- *Poor vision,* including narrowed peripheral vision, poor night vision, and sensitivity to bright lights
- *Hearing loss,* especially as it relates to the ability to hear warning sounds or sirens
- *Limited mobility or decreased flexibility,* which diminish response times and could limit the ability to turn your head
- *Chronic conditions,* such as rheumatoid arthritis, seizures, strokes, Parkinson's, sleep apnea, etc.
- *Medications,* which might cause drowsiness or have unpredictable or dangerous side-effects
- *Dementia,* which could make driving more confusing

Here are some signs that might indicate declining driving skills:
- Getting lost, even on familiar roads.
- The inability to follow directions.

- Erratic driving (abrupt lane changes, sudden braking/accelerating, hitting curbs, missing turns, and/or scaring pedestrians).
- Frequently startled, because drivers and pedestrians "appear out of nowhere".
- Having problems with night vision (even if the driver is more skilled in daylight hours).
- Unable to drive at the speed limit, particularly when driving on the freeway.
- Drifting into other lanes.
- Using turn signals inappropriately (This could mean they don't use them at all, or they keep them on without turning or changing lanes).
- Unable to look over the shoulder or difficulty changing gears (may be due to range of motion issues)
- Increased number of or begins receiving traffic tickets.
- Having at-fault accidents or near crashes (evidence can be noted through scrapes and dents on the mailbox and garage door, as well as on the vehicle).

Any of these warning signs could justify taking away the keys. They indicate that driving skills have diminished to a point where driving might be unsafe—to your loved one as well as anyone else on the road.

Though we all age differently, there are several factors that place older adults at significantly higher risk of accidents. And older adults are more likely to suffer serious injury than younger drivers involved in similar crashes.

Practical Suggestions

But...how can you tactfully take your aging parent's keys while still preserving dignity, independence and honor? Unfortunately, there is no easy answer, but we do have some practical suggestions.

<u>Be prepared.</u>
Though your parent may resist, become angry, and deny any decline in driving skill, YOU have to be the calming and reassuring influence. Expect an initial reaction of defensiveness. Be prepared to listen to your parent in a respectful manner.

What you might hear is fear. Your loved one realizes he/she is about to lose a major source of independence. It's natural to fight for the desire to go where he or she wants to go when they want to go there. Be prepared to reassure your parent that you're not trying to take away independence, but to provide ways to promote it so your parent can continue to enjoy a quality of life safely.

<u>Have a plan.</u>
Be prepared to discuss alternative transportation solutions that are least likely to be discarded out-of-hand. For example, if your parent has never used public transportation, it is unlikely that he or she will embrace the concept now. Point out not only his or her own jeopardy, but that of others on the road if they were to continue driving after it has become unsafe. Plan how to react if the conversation deteriorates (and it might) and how to approach it from a different angle at another time.

<u>Be an active listener.</u>
Show interest in what your parent has to say. Don't just hear their words, but understand their meaning. Don't interrupt. When they're finished speaking, show you understand correctly by restating his/her argument. Observe body language and other nonverbal cues, as these can be very telling.

<u>Show respect.</u>
Do not speak in a condescending manner, tone or volume. This will invariably create unneeded tension. Your parent is not a child and should not be treated as such.

<u>Discuss possible dangers.</u>
Your parent is an adult so there is no need to sugarcoat the dangers. Don't attempt to scare them. Rather, share your concern for their wellbeing and that of others who share the roads, including small children who might dart across a road to get a ball that's bounced into the street.

<u>Have options.</u>
Many private duty home care providers routinely take older adults to medical appointments, shopping, to the farmer's market and on other social outings in either our car or theirs. Your parents might have friends who are safe drivers who share interests and would be glad to have someone go with them to various activities—or even the grocery store. They might live in an assisted living facility that has regular transportation to various locations. With each option presented, be able to demonstrate how it empowers continued independence and quality of life.

Reassure independence.
Remind your parent that your desire is to explore ways in which he/she can continue to enjoy a good quality of life. Let your loved one know how much you value his/her independence. There may be other areas of daily activity that can be performed with ease. Focus on these areas while reassuring that changes in driving or transportation will enhance independence going forward.

There is no silver bullet answer in how to address such an emotionally charged issue as relinquishing the car keys. Our best advice is to be prepared, be patient and understanding, and reassure independence while introducing alternatives.

"Americans are broad-minded people. They'll accept the fact that a person can be an alcoholic, a dope fiend, a wife beater, and even a newspaperman, but if a man doesn't drive, there is something wrong with him."
~Art Buchwald

There's No Place Like Home

Chapter 15: Loneliness

One of the greatest benefits associated with home care—and perhaps the aspect that is most empowering—is companionship. When a caregiver has been carefully matched, the relationship between "caregiver" and "care recipient" can transform into that of "care partners."

Through the years, we have often found that underlying other issues or needs is loneliness.

Commonly, families believe that moving to a location where there are more people of the same generation is a solution for loneliness. Sometimes it is and sometimes it isn't. For example, when someone is moved into an assisted living facility, there are certainly many others who share similar ages. However, it could be shortsighted to think that simply because the ages are similar, the residents share common interests, desires, dislikes, etc. The reality is that though there might be common historical events that they've lived through, interests can vary widely.

Philosophers say that you die alone. Research indicates you might die earlier if you live a life of loneliness. We are all aware of the emotional pain associated with loneliness. It can be especially devastating to an older adult.

A recent study found that loneliness was a predictor of both functional decline and death. Researchers found that "loneliness is a common source of distress, suffering, and impaired quality of life in older persons."

We've observed great eagerness to discuss a patient's care needs, such as bathing, dressing/undressing, transferring, etc. We've witnessed the family's relief to discover that these needs can be met so efficiently. However, often their demeanor changes for the better when we shift to other areas like companionship.

I am always humbled and honored when given the opportunity to re-inject life into a lonely situation. Almost without exception, I have found that simply having someone share a meal or enjoy a game of Scrabble can have tremendously positive effects on a person's wellbeing. Most patients will just light up when I mention that we might also explore outings to the farmers market, a local exhibit or library, or just a trip to the mall. The key is in discovering their interests and empowering them to enjoy them.

Clearly, because of individual needs and abilities, discernment must be used to assess which outings are most appropriate for your loved one. For many people, the simple joy of a caregiver's company is enough to put a smile on their face.

I used to say that home care can't add days to your life, but it can add life to your days. In light of the research linking loneliness to functional decline and death, perhaps home care can do both!

Chapter 16: Why Wii?

Video games aren't just for kids. And, they aren't all "shoot 'em up" anymore either. To the contrary, many older adults are finding great benefit and pleasure through Wii games and a host of other online or video games.[1]

As you might guess from the chapter name, this chapter addressed Wii activities. However, the intent is to demonstrate that the possibilities are wide open with regard to physical and mental activity. Wii games are simply one avenue to consider.

Wii (pronounced "we") is a gaming console you can purchase for around $250 and easily connect to your television. Its wireless controllers are easy to use and come equipped with rubber grips and wrist straps to avoid slinging them across the room.

Wii games can be of benefit with older adults for several reasons. Unlike the types of games where you simply push buttons to shoot and move, these games

---

[1] Our hope is that this chapter is viewed as a "the sky is the limit" notion rather than an endorsement of any particular video game or activity.

engage the user in a physically active manner, simulating the real games. Most can easily accommodate multiple players, so the social activity and mental stimulation it provides is a bonus.

Some games are particularly beneficial to older adults—physically, cognitively and socially.

Wii Fit Plus can help older adults maintain fitness and balance. Some nursing homes have found that even those in wheelchairs can exercise and realize terrific therapeutic results from this program.

A favorite of many clients is the game of bowling found on Wii Sports. Even people in wheelchairs can enjoy it comfortably. In many assisted living facilities, this activity is becoming a mainstay—some have even formed bowling leagues within the facility!

Mental stimulation lowers the risk of developing Alzheimer's. The Alzheimer's Association promotes playing games as a good way to keep your brain active, and the AARP specifically recommends Big Brain Academy: Wii Degree "to keep your mind sharp." This game is designed as a virtual college that offers players a series of puzzles and math problems. The game is easy to play and allows up to eight people to participate at the same time.

Therefore, when you think of video games, you no longer need to conjure thoughts of young kids glued to their televisions instead of playing outside. Instead, think of these games as meaningful activities to engage older adults or aging parents in a fun and dynamic manner.

"In one thing you have not changed, dear friend," said Aragorn. "You still speak in riddles."
"What? In riddles?" said Gandalf. "No! For I was talking aloud to myself. A habit of the old: they choose the wisest person present to speak to; the long explanations needed by the young are wearying."
~ J.R.R. Tolkien, The Two Towers

There's No Place Like Home

Chapter 17: The Benefits of Bingo

Talk to the Activity Director at any skilled nursing facility and I'll bet you dollars to donuts that Bingo is a regular, and popular, activity.

The number of other meaningful activities older adults can engage in is limited only by one's imagination.

Until just a few years ago, my feeling was that Bingo was, at best, an activity simply designed to fill time and demonstrate a full "social calendar" for older adults. My thoughts were that it was patronizing to believe that Bingo would be the activity of first choice for older adults. After all, research has revealed that our interests actually increase with age.

So what is so special about Bingo? Why does it seem that so many older adults enjoy it? Is Bingo beneficial? As more research has been done, it appears that Bingo truly can be beneficial.

Concentration

Several research studies indicate that playing bingo can improve both concentration and short-term memory. The game is simple: the bingo caller announces a letter and number, you scan your game card for a match and you mark it when you find one. When you cover the appropriate design on your game card, you shout "Bingo!" However, because even a few seconds' delay can result in missed numbers you need careful concentration. Playing bingo regularly can help improve the kind of concentration that can be beneficial in other areas of daily living.

Coordination

If you don't believe the pace of a bingo game is fast, try calling it at a leisurely pace to a group of seasoned older adults. The caller must announce the numbers at a steady pace. Players must quickly and accurately scan their game card (or cards), processing what is heard and reacting with physical movement to mark the announced number. The reaction time must be quick. It takes coordination to react to the number, recognize matches and mark them appropriately. Therefore, Bingo can help improve older adults' coordination.

Stimulus

Because of the steady pace and required concentration, bingo is intellectually stimulating for older adults. Even when the winner's prizes are very simple, there is still excitement over the possibility of winning. This excitement can increase the release of endorphins. Endorphins stimulate people to feel elated during the game and relaxed afterward. Though the game might appear mundane or childish to some, do not underestimate the value of the stimulation realized by the players.

Social Benefits

Many older adults are, or feel, isolated from friends and family. Mobility challenges may preclude regular outings and family members may not visit as frequently as in the past. Therefore, participating in a bingo game can be a valuable social outlet. Beyond the benefits discussed above, the social interaction with other players and even spectators can be invaluable. While depression in older adults is a real and serious issue, participating in this type of social activity can be of great benefit by reducing the effects of depression.

Do not overlook the social, physical and cognitive value of bingo. It's a great game!

There's No Place Like Home

Chapter 18: Paying for Home Care

Most families pay for home care services out-of-pocket in the same way they would otherwise pay for residency (not rehabilitation) in a skilled nursing facility.

Funding options for home care include private pay, government assistance and insurance.

Private Pay
Many families pay for home care services out-of-pocket (termed private pay). This can be done through savings or existing income or a combination of the two. Being budget conscious myself, I urge families to carefully consider assets and income when making plans regarding both living and care arrangements.

Long-Term Care Insurance
This was developed specifically to cover the costs of long-term care services, most of which are not covered by traditional health insurance or Medicare. These include in-home services as well as care in a variety of facility and community settings.

Long-term care insurance policies have a benefit period or lifetime benefit maximum, which is the total amount of time or dollars up to which benefits will be paid. Common benefit periods for long-term care policies are two, three, four, or five years, and lifetime or unlimited coverage. Other options between five years and lifetime/unlimited coverage are also available from many companies. Most policies translate these time periods into dollar amounts and do not actually limit the number of days for which they will pay for care – just the maximum dollar amount the policy will pay.

See Chapter 20 for more information on Long Term Care insurance.

Medicare

Medicare is the federal program providing hospital and medical insurance to people aged 65 or older and to certain ill or disabled persons. Benefits may be available for home health care, but only if certain conditions are met. Additionally, Medicare may pay for up to 100 days of care in a skilled nursing facility per benefit period – 100% for the first 20 days (after a three-day hospital stay provided skilled care is needed). Beginning on day 21-100, Medicare requires a co-payment. To help cover the co-payment, many seniors may also have a Medicare supplemental insurance policy. In general, once Medicare stops paying for care, the supplemental payment will end as well.

A common notion is that Medicare will pay if you need to live in a nursing home. It will not. In fact, it will only pay for a brief period while a patient undergoes rehabilitation.

See Chapter 21 for more information about Medicare.

Medicaid
Generally, Medicaid pays for certain health services and nursing home care for those with low incomes and limited resources. Medicaid also pays for some long-term care services at home and in the community. Medicaid has limitations on the amount of assets you can own and the amount of income you may receive each month before you are eligible for benefits. Restrictions exist regarding the transfer of assets as well.

Medicaid is a common funding source for long-term care in a skilled nursing facility, but to be eligible for Medicaid, you must be nearly impoverished. In some circumstances, Medicaid pays for limited home care services, but again, you have to meet eligibility requirements.

Health Insurance
Traditional health insurance typically does not cover home care services.

Other Options
There are a number of other options such as taking out a line of credit on your home, securing a reverse mortgage to assess the equity in your home, and more. As with any options, there are pros and cons of doing so. To determine what might be best for your situation, you might speak with your financial and/or legal advisor to discuss these and other options.

There's No Place Like Home

Chapter 19: Long-Term Care Insurance

What is Long-Term Care Insurance? How does it work? What does it pay?

There are three key components to every Long Term Care insurance policy. Briefly, these include:
- Elimination Period — The "deductible" with the policy, it is represented by a period of time. It may be 30 days, 60 days, or 90 days, for instance. During this time period, the insured is responsible for paying for services provided.
- Daily/Weekly or Monthly Benefit — The policy benefit is defined as an amount of money available for approved services. The benefit may be defined by daily, weekly or monthly dollar figures, (e.g., $100/day or $3,500/month).
- Lifetime Maximum Benefit — The total amount the insurance company will pay over the entire duration of claims.

Other important information:
- What does the policy cover? Early policies only covered nursing home care, while today most policies cover other care options as well. See what settings your policy covers—skilled nursing facility, assisted living facility, or home.
- How much will it pay? Unlike Medicare, there is no uniformity in policies so it is important to know how much each policy pays.
- Will the policy pay for care provided by private individuals or does it need to be a private duty home care provider? It's not uncommon to find

much confusion in the general public about specific policies. Unless you are an insurance agent or financial planner, you might not have time to learn every detail about them. Our advice is to speak to your policy's representative to answer this question.

Since we frequently deal with these policies, your home care agency should be able to help. Ask if they have experience with your specific Long-Term Care insurance. Ask how they handle the claims process and if they handle all the required paperwork.

A good home care agency will serve as a guide through the maze of financial options.

Chapter 20: The 4 Parts of Medicare

Each of the four primary parts of Medicare addresses specific coverage. We refer to these as Part A, Part B, Part C and Part D coverage.

Part A covers hospital services, including semi-private rooms, meals, general nursing, drugs (as part of your inpatient treatment), and other hospital services and supplies. This includes the care you receive in acute care hospitals, critical access hospitals, inpatient rehabilitation facilities, long-term care hospitals, inpatient care as part of a qualifying clinical research study, and mental health care.

What isn't covered?
- Private-duty nursing
- Private room (unless medically necessary)
- Television and phone in your room (if there's a separate charge for these items)
- Personal care items, like razors or slipper socks

Part B covers services like doctor visits, lab tests, surgeries and supplies considered medically necessary to treat a disease or condition (such as wheelchairs or walkers).

Part C is a Medicare Advantage Plan. A Medicare Advantage Plan is a type of Medicare health plan offered by a private company that contracts with Medicare to provide you with all your Part A and Part B benefits. Most Medicare Advantage Plans offer prescription drug coverage, as well.

Part D is the Medicare prescription drug benefit. It is designed to subsidize the cost of prescription drugs.

What isn't covered?

Medicare doesn't cover everything. Even for the services covered by Medicare, you generally have to pay a deductible, coinsurance, and/or copayments.

Medicare generally will not cover:
- Long-term care
- Routine dental or eye care
- Dentures
- Cosmetic surgery
- Acupuncture
- Hearing aids and exams for fitting them
- Routine foot care

I hope this clarifies some of the confusion regarding Medicare coverage.

So remember, when exploring home care options or any long term care or housing options for a loved one, Medicare should probably not be included in your long term planning.

Chapter 21: Gifts for Caregivers

Caring for a loved one can be the most challenging task we face. Unlike the person who is difficult to shop for because she "has everything," caregivers need special attention. Consider the following gift ideas for family caregivers (as opposed to paid caregivers).

House Cleaning Service
Housekeeping can suffer when a family caregiver is burning the candle at both ends. Providing them with a house cleaning service is a welcome indulgence.

Entertainment Gift Card
Sometimes, a family caregiver needs time to turn off their cares, even if it is just for a few hours. You can purchase gift cards for restaurants, movie theaters, and a host of other fun places at most grocery stores. Make it personal. Offer to take their place, or arrange for a sitter to allow the caregiver to enjoy some R&R without worrying.

Day Spa Day
A completely self-indulgent experience is a rarity to someone who normally thinks of others first. Caregivers are often so busy meeting everyone else's needs that they overlook their own. A day of pure indulgence away from daily duties is usually much appreciated: massages, facials, manicures and pedicures make a perfect gift.

Netflix or Amazon
When getting away isn't feasible, or desired, pay for Netflix or Amazon. These are terrific resources for readers or those who enjoy a good movie, as time permits. A family caregiver will greatly appreciate the opportunity to enjoy a favorite book or movie.

Coupon for Respite
Create a Respite Coupon and offer to stay with their loved one for an afternoon or evening. Just like the Gift Cards, this will provide a few hours of "me" time for the caregiver. Even better, make a stipulation that the Coupon MUST be used during the most difficult time of day.

A Book of Encouragement
There are scores of books that are encouraging for caregivers. Here are just a few:
- Walking Together Through Illness: Twelve Steps for Caregivers and Care Receivers,
- The Overwhelmed Woman's Guide to…Caring for Aging Parents,
- Spiritual Care: A Guide for Caregivers,
- Twice Blessed: Encouragement for the Caregiver and the Carereceiver,
- Coping With Your Difficult Older Parent: A Guide for Stressed-Out Children.

A Note on Employees
Typically, employees of skilled nursing facilities, assisted living, and home care agencies are prohibited from accepting gifts. Sometimes, the best gift you can give your paid caregiver is a letter of appreciation. Express

your written appreciation to your caregiver, and send a copy of the letter to the agency.

Caregiving is a hard endeavor. Most caregivers, whether they are members of the family or paid professionals, feel largely unappreciated and/or taken for granted. Don't let that be the case for the special person who cares for your loved one.

There's No Place Like Home

Chapter 22: Veterans Benefits

The brave men and women of the United States Armed Forces have served our country faithfully for many years. As servicemen and women age, they may be eligible for veterans benefits related to home care.

What is Aid and Attendance?

The first benefit to be considered is the Aid and Attendance benefit. Unfortunately, many of the veterans who qualify for this benefit are nonetheless unaware that they qualify.

According to the U.S. Department of Veterans Affairs, "Veterans and survivors who are eligible for a VA pension and require the **aid and attendance** of another person, or are **housebound**, may be eligible for additional monetary payment. These benefits are paid in **addition** to monthly pension, and they are not paid without eligibility to Pension'" (http://www.benefits.va.gov/pension/aid_attendance_housebound.asp).

The Aid and Attendance benefit provides financial support to qualified veterans and their spouses to provide funds for specific costs that result from home care. Costs related to care in an assisted living facility or nursing home are also covered.

This benefit is paid in addition to the monthly pension that the veteran is already receiving; thus, the veteran must first be eligible for a monthly pension.

Aid and Attendance Qualifications

The Department of Veterans Affairs lists the conditions for eligibility to receive Aid and Attendance. One or more of these conditions must be met:
- The individual needs another person's aid in performing basic living functions, including bathing, eating, dressing, adjusting prosthetics, and more.
- The individual is bedridden.
- The individual is a patient in a nursing home.
- The individual's eyesight is slightly worse than clinical blindness.

In order to qualify for Aid and Attendance, the adjusted annual income of the veteran or surviving spouse must be beneath a certain income threshold. To view the current income thresholds, call the Veterans Administration at (800) 827-1000 or visit www.VA.gov. (As of this writing, you can access the income thresholds online by following these directions: Click "Benefits" on the home page of www.VA.gov. Next, select "Pension" on the left-hand navigation. From the drop-down menu that appears, select "Rates," and then click the "Rates: Veterans Pension" or "Rates: Survivors Pension" button.)

Applying for Aid and Attendance

If a veteran or the spouse of a veteran is already receiving a pension, they can simply write to the

Department of Veterans Affairs and say that they would like to apply for Aid and Attendance benefits. In order to expedite the process, it is best to include a statement from a licensed physician regarding the person's medical condition and the necessity of another's aid and attendance for them.

If the veteran or spouse is not already receiving a pension, the veteran or spouse must apply to receive pension benefits before applying to receive Aid and Attendance benefits. Be warned that the application process for pension benefits requires the completion of much paperwork.

The process of qualifying and applying for a pension or for Aid and Attendance can be very confusion. For assistance when applying, you can contact any of the following:
- The VA at (800) 827-1000 or www.VA.gov.
- National veterans' service organizations.
- A local veterans' services organization.

Elder law attorneys can often offer assistance to veterans or spouses of veterans who are applying for benefits. Additionally, home care agencies are often well acquainted with the process and can advise veterans who wish to apply. There are also national private organizations (such as Veterans Care Coordination) that specialize in assisting veterans.

There's No Place Like Home

Appendix 1: Licensing and Certification of Home Care Agencies

Each state determines licensure and certification requirements for home care providers. In some cases, these only pertain to agencies that serve Medicaid clients. Subcontractors require no licensure or certification, in most cases.

The breakdown for individual states is: 27 states have licensure but no certification requirements, one has certification but no licensure, 20 have no licensure or certification requirements, and three have both licensure and certification requirements.

States with Licensing but No Certification Requirements
- Colorado
- Connecticut
- District of Columbia
- Delaware
- Florida
- Georgia
- Illinois
- Indiana
- Louisiana
- Maryland
- Maine
- Minnesota
- North Carolina
- North Dakota
- Nebraska
- New Hampshire
- New Jersey

- Nevada
- New York
- Oklahoma
- Oregon
- Rhode Island
- Tennessee
- Texas
- Utah
- Virginia
- Washington

<u>States with No Licensing and No Certification Requirements</u>
- Alabama
- Arkansas
- Arizona
- California
- Hawaii
- Iowa
- Idaho
- Kansas
- Kentucky
- Michigan
- Missouri
- Mississippi
- Montana
- New Mexico
- Ohio
- South Dakota
- Vermont
- Wisconsin
- West Virginia
- Wyoming

States with both Licensing and Certification Requirements
- Massachusetts
- Pennsylvania
- South Carolina

State with No Licensing but Certification Requirement
- Alaska

There's No Place Like Home

Appendix 2: Glossary of Terms

Activities of Daily Living (ADLs)
Basic personal activities which include bathing, eating, dressing, mobility, transferring from bed to chair, and using the toilet. ADLs are used to measure a person's level of function.

Acute Disease
A disease characterized by a single episode of relatively short duration from which the patient returns to his/her normal or previous level of activity. While acute diseases are frequently distinguished from chronic diseases, there is no standard definition or distinction.

Acute Illness
A new illness that is usually short in duration and of sudden onset.

Admission
Date an individual is admitted into a facility or service (such as Hospice).

Adult Day Care
A daytime community-based program for functionally impaired adults providing a variety of health, social, and related support services in a protective setting.

Advance Care Planning
The process of discussing, determining and/or executing treatment directives and appointing a proxy decision maker regarding end of life preferences.

Advance Health Care Directive
A set of written instructions that a person gives that specify what actions should be taken for their health, if they are no longer able to make decisions due to illness or incapacity.

Adverse Drug Reaction (ADR)
An undesirable response associated with use of a drug that compromises therapeutic efficacy, enhances toxicity, or both.

Adverse Event
In a medical context, this is an injury resulting from a medical intervention.

Alzheimer's Disease
A progressive, irreversible disease characterized by degeneration of brain cells and loss of memory, causing the individual to become dysfunctional and dependent upon others for basic living needs.

Ambulatory Care
All types of health services which are provided on an outpatient basis, in contrast to services provided in the home or to persons who are inpatients in a facility. While many inpatients may be ambulatory, the term ambulatory care usually implies that the patient must travel to a location to receive services which do not require an overnight stay.

Area Agency on Aging (AAA)
A local (city or county) agency, funded under the federal Older Americans Act, that plans and coordinates various social and health service programs for persons 60 years of age or older. The network of AAA offices consists of more than 600 approved agencies.

Artificial Nutrition and Hydration
Artificial nutrition and hydration supplements or replaces ordinary eating and drinking by giving nutrients and fluids through a tube placed directly into the stomach (gastrostomy tube or G-tube), the upper intestine, or a vein.

Assisted Living
Residences that provide a "home with services" and that emphasize residents' privacy and choice. Residents typically have private locking rooms (only shared by choice) and bathrooms. Personal care services are available on a 24-hour-a-day basis.

A broad range of residential care services is provided which includes assistance with activities of daily living and often administration of medication. Assisted living facilities stress independence and generally provide less intensive care than that delivered in nursing homes and other long-term care institutions.

Assistive Devices
Tools that enable individuals with disabilities to perform essential job functions, e.g., telephone headsets,

adapted computer keyboards, enhanced computer monitors.

Behavioral Health
An umbrella term that includes mental health and substance abuse, and frequently is used to distinguish from "physical" health. Health care services provided for depression or alcoholism would be considered behavioral health care, while setting a broken leg would be physical health.

Beneficiary
An individual who receives benefits from (or is covered by) an insurance policy or other health care financing program.

Care Plan (Also called service plan or treatment plan.)
Written document which outlines the types and frequency of the long-term care services a consumer receives. It may include treatment goals for him or her for a specified time period.

Caregiver
Person who provides support and assistance with various activities to a client, family member, friend or neighbor. May provide emotional or financial support, as well as hands-on help with different tasks. Caregiving may also be accomplished from long distance.

Care/Case Management
Care/case management assesses clients' needs, creates service plans, and coordinates and monitors services; they may operate privately or may be employed by social service agencies or public

programs. Typically case managers are nurses or social workers.

Care/case management may also involve:
- The monitoring and coordination of treatment rendered to patients with specific diagnoses or requiring high-cost or extensive services.
- Procedures and processes used by trained service providers or a designated entity to assist children and families in accessing and coordinating services.

Certified Nurse Aide (CNA)
A nurse aide that has received certification by completing required state training and competency testing in appropriate skills.

Chronic Care
Care and treatment given to individuals whose health problems are of a long-term and continuing nature. Rehabilitation facilities, nursing homes, and mental hospitals may be considered chronic care facilities.

Chronic Disease
A disease that has one or more of the following characteristics: is permanent; leaves residual disability; caused by nonreversible pathological alteration; requires special training of the patient for rehabilitation; or requires a long period of supervision, observation, or care.

Chronic Illness
Long-term or permanent illness (e.g., diabetes, arthritis) which often results in some type of disability and which

may require a person to seek help with various activities.

Co-Morbidity
Condition that exists at the same time as the primary condition in the same patient (e.g., hypertension is a co-morbidity of many conditions such as diabetes, ischemic heart disease, end-stage renal disease, etc.).

Cognitive Impairment
Deterioration or loss of intellectual capacity which requires continual supervision to protect the insured or others, as measured by clinical evidence and standardized tests that reliably measure impairment in the area of, (1) short- or long-term memory, (2) orientation as to person, place and time, or (3) deductive or abstract reasoning. Such loss in intellectual capacity can result from Alzheimer's disease or similar forms of senility or irreversible dementia.

Continuing Care Retirement Community (CCRC)
Communities which offer multiple levels of care (independent living, assisted living, skilled nursing care) housed in different areas of the same community or campus and which give residents the opportunity to remain in the same community if their needs change. Provide residential services (meals, housekeeping, and laundry), social and recreational services, health care services, personal care, and nursing care. Require payment of a monthly fee and possibly a large lump-sum entrance fee. (Licensed as nursing homes/residential care facilities or as homes for the aging.)

Continuum of Care
The entire spectrum of specialized health, rehabilitative, and residential services available to the frail and chronically ill. Services focus on the social, residential, rehabilitative and supportive needs of individuals as well as needs that are essentially medical in nature.

Another use of this term is for clinical services provided during a single inpatient hospitalization or for multiple conditions over a lifetime. It provides a basis for evaluating quality, cost, and utilization over the long term.

Custodial Care
Care that does not require specialized training or services. (See also personal care.)

Dementia
Term which describes a group of diseases (including Alzheimer's Disease) which are characterized by memory loss and other declines in mental function.

Developmental Disability (DD)
A severe, chronic disability attributable to a mental or physical impairment or combination of mental and physical impairments; is manifested before the person attains age 22; is likely to continue indefinitely and results in substantial functional limitations. These occur in three or more of the following areas of major life activity: self-care, receptive and expressive language, learning, mobility, self-direction, capacity of independent living, and economic self-sufficiency. This reflects the person's need for a combination and sequence of special, interdisciplinary, or generic care

treatments and services, which are of lifelong or of extended duration and are individually planned and coordinated.

Discharge
The release of a patient from a provider's care, typically referring to the date at which a patient checks out of a hospital.

Do Not Resuscitate Order (Also called a DNR order, a No CPR order, a DNAR order, and an AND order)
A physician's order written in a patient's medical record indicating that health care providers should not attempt CPR or other heroic measures in the event of cardiac or respiratory arrest. In some regions, this order may be transferable between medical venues.

Durable Medical Equipment (DME)
Equipment such as a hospital bed, wheelchair, ventilator, oxygen system, home dialysis system, and/or prosthetics used at home. May be covered by Medicaid and in part by Medicare or private insurance. Prescribed by a physician for a patient's use for an extended period of time.

Estate Recovery
By law, states are required to recover funds from certain deceased Medicaid recipients' estates up to the amount spent by the state for all Medicaid services (e.g., nursing facility, home and community-based services, hospital, and prescription costs).

Geriatrician
A physician who is certified in the care of older people.

Gerontology
The study of the biological, psychological and social processes of aging.

Guardian
A judicially appointed overseer or conservator having authority to make health care decisions for an individual.

Home and Community-Based Services (HCBS)
Any care or services provided in a patient's place of residence or in a non-institutional setting located in the immediate community. HCBS may include home health care, adult day care or day treatment, medical services, or other interventions provided to allow a patient to receive care at home or in their community.

Home Health
Services provided at a patient's place of residence in compliance with a physician's written plan of care, usually reviewed every 60 days. These include nursing services, home health aide services, physical therapy, occupational therapy or speech pathology, and audiology services provided by a home health agency or by a facility licensed by the state to provide these medical rehabilitation services.

Home Health Agency (HHA)
A public or private organization providing home health services supervised by a licensed health professional in the patient's home either directly or through arrangements with other organizations.

Home Health Aide
A person who, under the supervision of a home health or social service agency, assists elderly, ill or disabled people with household chores, bathing, personal care, and other daily living needs. Social service agency personnel are sometimes called personal care aides.

Homemaker Services (Companion Care)
In-home help with meal preparation, shopping, light housekeeping, money management, personal hygiene, grooming, and laundry.

Hospice
A program which provides palliative and supportive care for terminally ill patients and their families, either directly or on a consulting basis with the patient's physician or another community agency. The whole family is considered the unit of care, and care extends through their period of mourning.

Hospice Care
Services for the terminally ill provided in the home, a hospital, or a long-term care facility. Includes home health services, volunteer support, grief counseling, and pain and symptom management.

Independent Living Facility
Rental units in which services are not included as part of the rent, although services may be available for purchase by residents for an additional fee.

Instrumental Activities of Daily Living (IADLs)
Household/independent living tasks which include using the telephone, taking medications, money

management, housework, meal preparation, laundry, and grocery shopping.

Intubation
Refers to "endotracheal intubation," the insertion of a tube through the mouth or nose into the trachea (windpipe) to create and maintain an open airway to assist breathing.

Long-Term Care Insurance (LTCI)
Insurance policies that pay for long-term care services (such as nursing home and home care) that Medicare and Medigap policies do not cover. Policies vary in terms of what they will cover, and may be expensive. Coverage may be denied based on health status or age.

Medicaid (Title XIX)
Federal and state-funded program of medical assistance to low-income individuals of all ages. There are income eligibility requirements for Medicaid.

In addition, State Medicaid programs may use functional criteria for coverage of nursing home services, home health services, personal care services, home and community-based waiver services, and other Medicaid-covered services. Two levels of disability criteria may be applied--one to determine overall Medicaid eligibility and one to determine eligibility for specific covered services.

Medicare Supplement Insurance (MedSupp) (Also called Medigap)
Insurance supplement to Medicare that is designed to fill the "gaps" left by Medicare (such as co-payments). May pay for some limited long-term care expenses, depending on the benefits package purchased.

Nursing Home
Facility licensed by the state to offer residents personal care as well as skilled nursing care on a 24 hour a day basis. Provides nursing care, personal care, room and board, supervision, medication, therapies and rehabilitation. Rooms are often shared, and communal dining is common. (Licensed as nursing homes, county homes, or nursing homes/residential care facilities.)

Occupational Therapy (OT)
Therapy designed to help patients improve their independence with activities of daily living through rehabilitation, exercises, and the use of assistive devices. May be covered in part by Medicare.

Older Americans Act (OAA)
Federal legislation that specifically addresses the needs of older adults in the United States. Provides funding for aging services (such as home-delivered meals, congregate meals, senior center, employment programs). Creates the structure of federal, state, and local agencies that oversee aging services programs.

Palliative Care (Also called comfort care)
A comprehensive approach to treating serious illness that focuses on the physical, psychological, and spiritual needs of the patient. Its goal is to achieve the

best quality of life available to the patient by relieving suffering, controlling pain and symptoms, and enabling the patient to achieve maximum functional capacity. Respect for the patient's culture, beliefs, and values is an essential component.

Personal Care (Also called custodial care)
Assistance with activities of daily living as well as with self-administration of medications and preparing special diets.

Personal services such as bathing and toileting (and sometimes expanded to include light housekeeping), furnished to an individual who is not an inpatient or a resident of a group home, assisted living facility, or long-term facility such as a hospital, nursing facility, intermediate care facility for the mentally handicapped, or an institution for mental disease. Personal care services are those that individuals would typically accomplish themselves if they did not have a disability.

Physical Therapy (PT)
Therapy designed to restore/improve movement and strength in people whose mobility has been impaired by injury and disease. May include exercise, massage, water therapy, and assistive devices. May be covered in part by Medicare.

Program of All-Inclusive Care for the Elderly (PACE)
A managed care plan that coordinates Medicare and Medicaid acute care and long-term care for dual eligible enrollees (those age 55 and older, living in a PACE area, and otherwise eligible for nursing home

care). A capitated payment mechanism is used for PACE plan enrollees.

Respite Care
Service in which trained professionals or volunteers come into the home to provide short-term care (from a few hours to a few days) for an older person to allow caregivers some time away from their caregiving role.

Special Care Units
Long-term care facility units with services specifically for persons with Alzheimer's Disease, dementia, head injuries, or other disorders.

Spend-Down
Medicaid financial eligibility requirements are strict, and may require beneficiaries to spend down (use up) assets or income until they reach the eligibility level.

Appendix 3: Questions to Ask When Choosing a Home Care Company

- How long has your agency been providing home care services?

- (If required) Is your agency licensed by the state?

- What range of home care services does your agency provide?

- How do you select and train your employees?

- Do you perform background checks on staff?

- Is care documented, detailing the specific tasks to be carried out by each professional caregiver?

- Is there a supervisor(s) to oversee the quality of care that is received? If so, how often do these individuals make visits?

- Who can we call with questions or complaints?

- How do you follow up on and resolve problems?

- Will the same caregiver be with my loved one on each visit?

- Do you conduct an in-home assessment and what does that include?

- Can you coordinate other types of services and supports?

- What are your financial procedures? Deposit? Billing cycle?

- Do you furnish written statements explaining all of the costs and payment plan options associated with the home care services you provide?

- What procedures are in place to handle emergencies?

- Are services available 24 hours a day, seven days a week?

Other Notes:

There's No Place Like Home

About The Author

Greg was born and raised in the town of Nutley, New Jersey. He graduated from Nutley High School and went on to attend Rutgers University. He has lived in New Jersey for all of his life and currently resides in south Jersey. He has three children (two boys and a girl) and one granddaughter.

Greg has a private pilot's license, having considered aviation as a career earlier in his life. He loves fishing, especially fresh water fishing—even though he lives ten minutes from the ocean. He also enjoys gardening and working in the yard.

Greg and wife Phebe

Greg is very active in his church. The rest of his free time is spent providing high-quality care to clients throughout south Jersey as the owner of Angel Alliance Caregivers.

You can contact Greg at:

Angel Alliance Caregivers

Physical Address:
703 West White Horse Pike
Galloway, New Jersey 08205

Mailing Address: P.O. Box 242
Cologne, New Jersey 08213

Phone: 609-965-0028

Website: AngelAllianceCaregivers.com

Email: Greg@AngelAllianceCaregivers.com

Made in the USA
Columbia, SC
31 May 2024